Biblical
Concepts for
Christian
Counseling

Biblical Concepts for Christian Counseling

A Case for Integrating Psychology and Theology

William T. Kirwan

BAKER BOOK HOUSE

Grand Rapids, Michigan 49506

Copyright © 1984 by Baker Books
a division of Baker Publishing Group
P.O. Box 6287, Grand Rapids, MI 49516-6287
www.bakerbooks.com

Library of Congress Card Number: 84-70193

ISBN 10: 0-8010-5454-0
ISBN 978-0-8010-5454-9

Fourteenth printing, August 2007

Printed in the United States of America

To the women in my life . . .

Anne
Suzanne
Agatha, Kathleen, Vivienne, and **Julia**

Each of you walks through the pages of my life and each of you in your own way has helped me to look to a yonder hill and there see Him who alone brings personality and life to completion, even Jesus, the Author and Finisher of our faith. Thanks always.

Contents

Foreword

The relationship between psychology and theology has become an issue of increasing concern in recent years for the Christian community. Twenty-five years ago there was only a small trickle of evangelical books and articles on this topic. Now the trickle has become a steady stream. It continues to expand, being reinforced by the *Journal of Psychology and Theology,* the *Journal of Psychology and Christianity,* the Christian Association for Psychological Studies, two Christian doctoral programs in clinical psychology, and master's programs in counseling at almost every evangelical seminary. However, the quality of publication on the relationship of psychology and theology has not always kept pace with the quantity.

One reason for the lack of quality and of substantive integration of theology and psychology has been the failure of theologians to participate in this task. In 1976 David Carlson of Trinity College and Seminary publicly called for the involvement of theologians. Apparently theologians either did not hear the call or did not heed it, but psychologists with theological training did. In the eight years since Carlson's call there have been several significant works by theologically trained psychologists. William Kirwan's work represents the cutting edge of this high-quality response.

While it is still too soon to call the present volume the definitive work on the topic, it is clearly one of the most substantive. First, Dr. Kirwan believes Scripture and theology have something to contribute to the disciplines of psychological pathology and counseling. Second, his discussion evidences a sophisticated understanding of psychological theory as well as theology. Third, he not only synthesizes the creative insights of theologians and psychologists, but shows he understands the unity of God's truth which is contained in psychology and theology, that is, in general and special revelation.

Dr. Kirwan is eminently qualified for the task of relating theology and psychology. He holds earned doctorates in Christian ministry and clinical psychology. He was a pastor for almost ten years; currently he teaches pastoral counseling at the seminary level and also conducts a private practice in psychotherapy. It has been a privilege to dialogue with Dr. Kirwan while he was developing this book. I can only hope the reader will be as stimulated by its ideas as I have been.

John D. Carter
La Mirada, California
June, 1984

Preface

In *Biblical Concepts for Christian Counseling,* William Kirwan provides for us an excellent introduction to a subject that seldom gets such a well-balanced and judicious treatment. The book is a delight to read. In part this is true because it deals with a difficult subject in very readable English with no attempt to impress the intelligent lay person with technical jargon that at best is a short-cut only for those already in the know and at worst is a pretense of scholarship that serves as a mask for immense ignorance. The author approaches his subject in a businesslike fashion and writes with clarity and deftness that show he knows what he is talking about.

The special value of the volume lies in its balanced wisdom. William Kirwan takes very seriously both his Christianity and his psychology. Unlike some evangelicals who have presumed to dabble in psychology, he does not attempt to heal mental illness with a verse of Scripture and a call to repentance. Neither does he appropriate secular psychologies of the day—either "pop" or serious—baptize them with Christian vocabulary and a syrup of piety, and then pawn them off as "Christian psychology." Rather he displays a solid understanding of the basic secular and non-evangelical psychologies prevalent on today's market and shows how they have been built on false or inadequate presuppositions. Then patiently he builds his own psychology, which is based on biblical presuppositions but also draws critically from a wide background of modern psychologies and contemporary counseling theory. He acknowledges the validity of psychology as a science and justifies his critical use of its insights on the solid grounds of a valid natural revelation (clearly recognized in Scripture) and the common grace of God.

Throughout the volume William Kirwan manifests a reverent dependence upon Scripture and a sharply defined perception of the basic doctrines of evangelical faith. Here his solid theological education preserves him from many foolish mistakes into which other evangelicals have usually fallen when they have sought to write on psychology and religion. Kirwan's exegesis is sober and faithful to the text. He is solidly committed to the biblical doctrines of man, human sin, and personal regeneration. Obviously they are not theological appendages from a religion kept in isolation from his understanding of psychology and counseling, but an inherent aspect of his total viewpoint. Here, for example, we find a balanced handling of the biblical teaching on self-esteem, much needed on the contemporary scene. By recognizing the importance of the self in the biblical teaching on the human personality and by setting this truth in its proper biblical context (the creation, the fall, and redemption), he preserves the biblical view of sin. Popular radio and television preachers who proclaim a "gospel of self-esteem" without any conviction of sin or any biblical call to repentance badly need to read the balanced presentation in this book.

In short, William Kirwan has produced a solid piece of work. *Biblical Concepts for Christian Counseling* will prove a wise and safe guide for those seeking to thread their way through the land mines of modern psychological theory. With its help they can build for themselves a truly Christian understanding of psychology, carefully grounded on biblical presuppositions and yet alert and receptive to truth gleaned from modern research. The volume is also a practical guide for the Christian counselor who wishes to avail himself of the valid insights of contemporary practice.

Kenneth S. Kantzer
Deerfield, Illinois
July, 1984

Acknowledgments

How does one adequately acknowledge contributions to a book which is in reality the result of a lifetime? Many people who have impacted my life and significantly contributed to these pages will be overlooked and inadvertently omitted. To them I want to say thanks, for in the hustle of time they have been overlooked but not forgotten.

First, my thanks to John Sanderson, John Carter, Steve Smallman, and David Jones—all of whom have been superb students of the doctrines of grace and each in his own way an astute student of human behavior. My dialogue and discussion with these men have formulated a great part of the contents of this book. Also, for their contributions through lectures and books, I would be remiss not to acknowledge Bruce Narramore and William Oglesby, whose ideas have also significantly influenced my thinking.

Secondly, I must acknowledge those who have contributed to the more clinical side of my thinking. Among them are Gene Holemon, a psychiatrist and close friend from whom I never cease to glean new thoughts both clinically and theologically. And Alan Plotkin, my original mentor and supervisor, who gave so freely of himself, both to me and to the Christian Counseling Service of Randallstown, Maryland. Also I would be remiss without mentioning Robert A. Miller for originally encouraging me as a young pastor to become more interested in my own suffering and the suffering lives of others, and to become an agent for healing and change.

To acknowledge all those who have contributed spiritually to my life would be impossible, but I must acknowledge Billy Graham, Ralph Kidwell, Verna Wright, Murray Smoot, and Edmund Clowney, all of whom were God's human instruments in my finding Christ and being "rooted and grounded in Him."

Thanks also to my friends and colleagues on the faculties of Covenant Theological Seminary and Trinity Evangelical Divinity School, and especially to Robert Rayburn, whose example of godly faith and personal fatherly affirmation have extended the feelings of worth my own father instilled in me years ago.

To the board of trustees of Covenant Seminary for their constant trust and gentle exhortation over the last ten years, especially Jim Orders, Art Stoll, and Lanny Moore. They can no longer ask, "When is the book coming out?"

Then to the session and members of the Liberty Reformed Presbyterian Church for their vision of seeing the aid that the ministry of counseling can be in both evangelism and sanctification. We labored together for ten years; and as time gathers us in, I must honor you all for allowing your young pastor to venture out into a new and untried direction, but especially my thanks go to Charles Klein, Bill O'Rourke, and Charles Lathe for their personal friendship and support.

Also I must acknowledge hundreds of doctoral and master's-level students who have contributed to making my thinking more Christian. So many of you contributed that I cannot begin to mention you. A special note of thanks must go to my teaching assistants through the years, especially to now Professor Dick Cole and to Dane Ver Merres for his part in aiding his disorganized professor and friend.

Finally, to those who have labored so diligently in getting all these thoughts in readable form. You had the worst of writers to work with. To Mary Grace O'Rourke and Karen D. Arezzo for their constant encouragement and help in the original writing of this manuscript, and also to Dan Van't Kerkhoff, Betty DeVries, and Ray Wiersma for their forbearance and patience in formulating and finalizing publication.

A special note of thanks to two esteemed colleagues, John Carter and Kenneth Kantzer, for writing the foreword and the preface.

PART ONE

Christianity and Psychology

1

The Four Basic
Counseling Positions

My wife Anne has a close friend who had to be hospitalized not long ago for fear that she might commit suicide. For thirteen years she has been handicapped by chronic depression, destructive relationships, feelings of worthlessness, lack of confidence. A talk I had with her before her hospitalization convinced me that she has a firm commitment to Christ and the Bible, even though she finds it difficult to trust the Lord on a daily basis. She said she has never been able to fully trust anyone.

How can a person with strong Christian convictions, a person who has experienced love and prayer among other believers, and participated in Bible studies and the fellowship of a vital church, fall apart? When such an event occurs, what is the effect on the cause of Christ? Does it invalidate the Christian faith? Does it cast doubt on Christ's power to restore people to mental health? Anne wondered if those Christians who offer simplistic answers could even begin to understand the complexity of our friend's problem.

A lot of confusion exists about how Christianity relates to mental health. Through my work as a minister and psychologist, I have discovered that there are basically four views of the relationship between Christianity and psychology and, accordingly, four basic counseling positions.

One psychologist friend—with outstanding professional credentials—believes "religion" to be good and worthwhile. He contends, however, that empiricism and the laws of psychology rank above the essential elements of the Christian faith. Religion, if it fits into the process of aiding a patient's ability to cope with problems, is acceptable but not essential. While biblical concepts may occasionally be of some value in the therapeutic process, they must never be allowed to interfere with its basic course. This view, which I will call the *un-Christian view*, is probably held by a majority of mental-health professionals. They are likely to insist that religion, or more specifically biblical Christianity, has nothing to offer individuals like our depressed friend. Some would even contend that Christianity caused or contributed to some of her problems.

On the other hand, I know a pastoral counselor who looks at all emotional disturbances as spiritual problems. He believes that all depression and despair result from violating certain scriptural principles. He argues that obeying God's Word is the answer to all mental problems. He considers repentance and confession of conscious sin the key to healing. I call this the *spiritualized view*. I held this position while I was in seminary and I argued vehemently for it. I remember reading Gilbert Little's *Nervous Christians* several times in my college years. According to the author, "when Christ enters into the individual's soul and self is crucified, the symptom complex common to nervous patients will not develop in textbook style, because the Christian then goes in the power of Christ instead of self." In spite of its kernel of truth, Little's outlook now seems to me to be simplistic and incompatible with both psychological and biblical data. I know from experience, including personal therapy, that spiritualized answers like that, given to suffering Christians with real problems, are actually cruel and heartless. Moreover, the Bible speaks often about mental suffering as a reality of life.

A third counselor represents the *parallel view*. He believes in the principles of psychology and is skilled in their application. He knows Christ in a real way and understands the Bible well, yet there is little overlap between his Christianity and psychology. Each seems to function independently of the other, so that biblical words like "sin," "guilt," and "faith" are replaced in the counseling office by terms like "acting out," "intropunitive reaction," and "obsession." Counselors who stress data from both the Bible and science, but do not integrate them, are closer to the truth than are either of the first two counselors I mentioned, yet something is amiss in their approach.

Finally, I think of a fourth counselor. He also has a vast appreciation of psychology and skill in its application as well as a serious commitment to Christ and the Bible. But he holds an *integrated view*, which does not see the Bible and psychology as functioning independently in different spheres. This counselor has an ability to put together the truths of psychology and the Bible in a harmonious way. I admire his gift for showing how psychological understanding can often enlighten a great biblical truth.

Biblical Christianity and psychology, when rightly understood, do not conflict but represent functionally cooperative positions. By taking both spheres into account, a mental-health professional can help Christians avoid the inevitable results of violating psychological laws structured into human personality by God. Our suicidal friend was exposed to all four approaches. She found lasting help, however, only from a counselor who used an integrative approach. Therefore, it seems to be incumbent on psychologists in the evangelical camp to integrate their counseling theories and methods with the Word of God. At present only a few counselors seem able to combine the two.

In Part One of this book I will examine in greater detail each of the four positions mentioned above and demonstrate that the integrated view is the best. Indeed, the biblical presentation itself virtually demands that the data of psychology and of Scripture be integrated. In Part Two I will endeavor to present a theological perspective integrating psychology and Scripture, including a discussion of the fall and our experience of its emotional consequences today. In Part Three I will present my own model for counseling, which I believe thoroughly integrates psychological theory with God's Word.

The Necessity of Identifying Presuppositions

To critique the four basic views of the relationship between Christianity and psychology, we must make a clear assessment of the differences between these views and of their individual strengths and weaknesses. But before we can do that, we must identify the presuppositions underlying each of the four basic counseling positions.

Each person's overall world-view rests on a presupposition or basic assumption. Francis Schaeffer defines presupposition as "a belief or theory which is assumed before the next step in logic is developed. Such a prior postulate then consciously or unconsciously affects the way a person subsequently reasons" (Schaeffer 1968, 179). Through careful analysis, each person's philosophy or belief system, however elaborate, can be traced back to a clearly defined starting point or presupposition.

All counseling theories have philosophical presuppositions at their core. Those basic assumptions lead to certain logical conclusions concerning the human person, behavioral change, and meaning in life.

The operation of presuppositions is illustrated in Figure 1. "Physical reality" refers to the natural world, which can be studied scientifically. "Observed data" are the facts noted about that world, ranging from casual impressions during a lunch discussion to observation of cells under a microscope or clinical notations of the thoughts and emotions of an individual being counseled. The observed data are then interpreted according to the observer's unique thought patterns or constructs, and the interpreted data are fed into his "world-view," which is based on his fundamental presuppositions. The interpreted data reinforce and further solidify the world-view by expanding its horizons and complexity. But in turn, "feedback" from the world-view influences the interpretative processes and hence the assimilation of data.

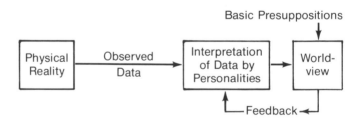

FIGURE 1   **The Operation of Presuppositions** (based on a figure in David L. Dye, *Faith and the Physical World* [Grand Rapids: Eerdmans, 1966], p. 71)

In practice, we select the data and interpretations that best suit our world-view, and that world-view, in turn, is rooted in our presuppositions. Only those who fail to understand the circularity of the process could ever assert that a particular world-view is scientifically proven. The presuppositions at the foundation of every world-view are beyond the ability of science to prove or disprove.

Clearly, one's world-view is determined not simply by data input, but also by whatever basic presuppositions underlie the entire process. The process is circular, starting and finishing with the underlying presuppositions as one attempts to make both old and new data compatible with one's presuppositions. Philosopher Michael Polanyi emphasized that the inherent structure of the "act of knowing makes us both necessarily participate in its shaping and acknowledge its results with universal intent" (Polanyi 1964, 65). Walter Thorson sums up Polanyi's major thesis: "There is no knowledge apart from the knower's, and the personal participation of the knower in that which he knows is both pervasive and inescapable" (Thorson 1969, 41).

Astronomer Robert Jastrow has described the reluctance of some leading astronomers to accept the evidence that the universe originated with a "big bang." Their presupposition that there is no God seems to be influencing their scientific outlook. Jastrow points out that their response is based on emotions, not evidence:

> There is a strange ring of feeling and emotion in [their reactions]. They come from the heart, whereas you would expect the judgments to come from the brain. . . . As usual when faced with trauma, the mind reacts by ignoring the implications. . . . For the scientist who has lived by his faith in the power of reason, the story ends like a bad dream. He has scaled the mountain of ignorance; he is about to conquer the highest peak; as he pulls himself over the final rock, he is greeted by a band of theologians who have been sitting there for centuries. [Jastrow 1978, 113–16]

Jastrow's article illustrates Polanyi's thesis that, in part, personal internal or subjective thought patterns will be superimposed on the external data and the objective world. That kind of participation of the knower is, quietly and subtly, a major part of knowing; it rests on commitment to certain postulates the knower holds to be true.

Thus, data do not exist as neutral or brute facts but are always interpreted by the observer. For example, a theist who discovers a fact interprets it as a God-created fact; an atheist interprets the same fact as a non-God-created fact. Agnosticism is a difficult position to hold consistently, since brute facts cannot be perceived or understood without being interpreted in accordance with some kind of world-view. Because data must necessarily be interpreted, even the most scientific psychological investigation is a highly human activity drawing on the conscious and unconscious personality, interests, ideals, and aspirations of the observer.

The Presuppositions of Science and Christianity

Before we can identify the presuppositions underlying the four basic views of the relationship between psychology and Christianity, we must determine the presuppositions of psychology (the science of mental processes and behavior) and of Christianity. Both science as a discipline and the mindset of the scientist who practices the art rest on specific presuppositions. Edwin Burtt pointed out in his *Metaphysical Foundations of Modern Science* that an individual cannot operate as a scientist, cannot put on a white coat and go into a laboratory, without taking along at least three basic assumptions. First, scientists presuppose reality. They believe that the world is real and observable, that it can be studied, and that through such research legitimate data are achievable. Second, scientists presuppose causality: some type of causal law applies throughout the whole of reality. Some causal relationship exists between the various states of the universe. The principle of causality means that every state of the universe is related to all other states of the universe. A third assumption scientists make is that physical reality and the human mind's verification of that reality are logical and rational. If the human mind were not logical and rational, science could not study physical reality.

Obviously, atheists and other non-Christians have investigated nature. But on what basis can such scientists assert that the world is real, that what is observed as reality today will be reality tomorrow? For atheists, the basic assumption is that the world is here by chance, that a fortuitous collision of molecules is responsible for the universe, the earth, and human beings. ("Chance" is used here as a philosophical term denoting purposeless randomness, not as a scientific term denoting the mathematical probability of a certain event.) How can an individual whose basic assumption is that the world is a chance occurrence assert that the universe is constant and consistent?

On the other hand, those that believe that God exists and that He is the maker and sustainer of the universe do have a firm basis for scientific work. Christians can assert: "It is possible for human beings to observe nature because God has made it and it is real. We can assume causality, because God has created a consistent world with cause and effect built in. Further, God has made the human person capable of logical thought, which can be applied not only in matters of science but also in other areas of human endeavor."

Christians also believe that reality extends beyond what can be observed and measured. Christians believe in a personal God who has revealed Himself in Scripture. The spiritual and psychological assertions of Scripture are true, although many of them cannot be scientifically examined. The Christian world-view includes spiritual and psychological dimensions beyond the observable physical reality.

The Christian world-view is depicted in Figure 2. Note that while the Christian world-view goes beyond the scientific world-view (presuppositions 4 and 5), the first three presuppositions are the same. Therefore, the Christian can legitimately make use of and build upon the findings of secular scientists. The doctrine of common grace states that God's favor and goodness are showered on all people; He endows everyone with intellect, reason, and talents. People are able to function in God's world because He is good, even though they may hold Him in contempt or even hate Him.

Yet in our century the evangelical church has tended to deny any validity to psychological findings because of its adverse reaction to various philosophical interpretations by Sigmund Freud, Carl Rogers, B. F. Skinner, and others. The fact is that although their philosophical conclusions are doubtless anti-Christian, their empirical findings are not. Whether or not they acknowledge that human personality is made in the image of God, the fact remains

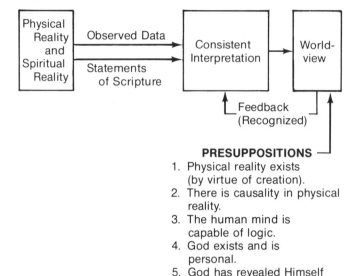

FIGURE 2   The Christian World-View (based on a figure in Dye, *Faith and the Physical World*, p. 76)

that they have made a thorough study of personality. Recognizing that God reveals Himself not only in the Bible through special revelation, but also through general revelation, we can accept the findings of non-Christian scientists to the extent that their non-Christian presuppositions have not colored the truth discovered.

Francis Schaeffer, a leading philosopher of our day, sounds this note in his insistence that "not all science is junk." Schaeffer is following the lead of Cornelius Van Til, who in his younger days stressed that non-Christian scientists using Christian presuppositions ("borrowed capital" he called them) bring to light "a great deal of truth about the facts and laws of the universe. . . . And as Christians, we may and should make grateful use of truth, from whatever source it springs, because ultimately all truth springs from God" (Van Til 1940, 38). Thirty years later Van Til still consistently held this position:

> As far as the principle of interpretation is concerned, the natural man makes himself the final point of reference. So far, then, as he carries through his principle, he interprets all things *without God.*

In principle he is hostile to God. But he cannot carry through his principle completely. He is restrained by God from doing so. Being restrained by God from doing so, he is enabled to make contributions to the edifice of human knowledge. The forces of creative power implanted in him are to some extent released by God's common grace. *He therefore makes positive contributions to science in spite of his principles and because both he and the universe are the exact opposite of what he, by his principles, thinks they are.* [Van Til 1969, 22]

John Calvin in the *Institutes of the Christian Religion* (2.2.15–16) also made a strong case for accepting the truth discovered by the sciences:

Therefore in reading profane authors, the admirable light of truth displayed in them should remind us that the human mind, however much fallen and perverted from its original integrity, is still adorned and invested with admirable gifts from its Creator. If we reflect that the Spirit of God is the only fountain of truth, we will be careful, as we would avoid offering insult to him, not to reject or condemn truth wherever it appears. . . . If the Lord has been pleased to assist us by the work and ministry of the ungodly in physics, dialectics, mathematics and other similar sciences, let us avail ourselves of it.

On the other hand, Christians should not automatically react positively to everything published by psychologists, saying that "all truth is God's truth." Many non-Christian psychologists (e.g., Skinner) take empirical data (which can be verified) and go on to make metaphysical or philosophical statements (which cannot be proved). Such philosophizing falls beyond the discipline of the science itself.

The Presuppositions of the Four Basic Counseling Positions

Now that we have identified the basic presuppositions of Christianity and science (and hence of psychology), we can briefly consider the presuppositional foundations of the four counseling positions described at the beginning of this chapter (and outlined in detail by John Carter, 1977). The *un-Christian view* makes the basic epistemological assumption that human reason is the ultimate source of truth. The first counselor mentioned believes that psychology is more fundamental, comprehensive, and technically useful than any supposed divine revelation.

Among those who view the human person rather than God as the ultimate source of truth, there is great diversity. At one end of the continuum is the militant atheist or materialist who believes that everything is just matter, including human beings, who are nothing more than an accidental collision of atoms and molecules. In this extreme view religion, because it is unscientific, has a detrimental effect on society. The materialist or atheist says that religion harms human beings by inhibiting free expression within society, especially sexual expression. Logically, such an ideology leaves the human person with no values, purpose, or morals.

In the view of the atheist, a session between counselor and counselee amounts to nothing more than one "product of chance" trying to help another "product of chance" to live "normally." A psychologist who holds this basic position wrote a lengthy book about Richard Speck, who murdered eight nurses in Chicago in 1966. The psychologist presented the thesis that Speck as a product of chance was unable to do anything except murder the nurses. Francis Schaeffer pointedly asks how this outlook treats the eight women. The answer is that it makes them the victims of chance; the whole tragedy reduces to nothing but chance. Schaeffer then asks what effect such an outlook has on society. Philosophically, it forces society to accept any neurotic or psychotic behavior. Without values there can be no personal accountability for actions. And what does this outlook make of Speck himself, Schaeffer finally asks. It makes him less than human because he is regarded as having ceased to function and exist as a man who has values or purpose (Schaeffer 1969, 103–04).

Thus, in being consistent with their basic beliefs, atheistic psychologists put themselves into a strait jacket. Their presuppositions prevent them from establishing firm goals and guidelines in counseling.

Counselors who believe that God exists but deny that He is personal are at the other end of the un-Christian view. Such individuals do not take a militant stand against Christianity or religion, but still affirm that the human person is the source of truth and knowledge. In their view, religions may be a deterrent to personal growth, so they assert that emotional problems are better solved by applying principles of emotional maturity and by improving interpersonal relationships. Psychologists who believe that God exists but deny that He is relevant or that He concerns Himself with the problems of His people might well be asked about the basic reference point of their therapy. Jean-Paul Sartre rightfully said that finite persons need an infinite reference point outside themselves in order to find themselves. If God is not personal, then He cannot relate to us and we are left on our own. What kind of means could then enable us to rise above the inner workings of our psyche and thereby relate to God or to the cosmos? We would be left with no reference point by which to establish guidelines and goals for counseling except that of other people.

In the same vein are psychologists who verbally assent that God is personal—that He can work in people's lives and in history—but do not live out that belief. Their counseling is generally devoid of reference to God, and thus makes no claim or use of guidance from God. Such counselors are, in fact, practical atheists who have cut themselves and their clients off from spiritual guidance.

The *spiritualized view* holds that revelation supersedes reason and may be contrary to reason. By assuming, say, that all emotional disturbances are the result of violating biblical principles, such counselors limit themselves to spiritual truth, neglecting or ignoring other truth that is also God's truth. Their position denies the doctrine of common grace. Their blatant repudiation of psychological truth which comes from non-Christian sources (e.g., humanists and existentialists) is in direct opposition to the views of Calvin, Van Til, and Schaeffer. Would the spiritualizers apply their key principle to God-created physical laws in the same way they do to God-created psychological laws? To do so would mean asking the druggist if the discoverer of a prescribed drug was a Christian, or determining if the surgeon recommended to perform a needed operation on a Christian patient is a believer.

Christians believe that the Bible has the ultimate answers to our meaning and purpose in life and agree that God is a necessary personal reference point if we are to function in a meaningful way. At the same time, the Bible is not a medical textbook. Human beings have been endowed by God with the ability to develop and use the science of medicine, but we must go beyond pure spiritual teaching to do so. Certain psychological as well as physical laws are part of our makeup and cannot be ignored as though they have no relevance to our well-being.

To hold that such problems as mental distress, depression, and anxiety are always the result of disobedience to God's commandments, or the result of some conscious sin that an individual is harboring, is unfair and perhaps even cruel to a suffering person. Counselors see many fine and sincere Christians who are bowed down by false guilt, depressions, and anxieties which are not the result of any sin or wrongdoing on their part. Their emotional difficulty may well be the result of someone else's not having followed God's laws. Many times the counselee is more sinned against than sinning.

The *parallel view* accepts both reason and revelation as relevant in counseling. Counselors espousing this view hold to a firm Christian position and at the same time make use of psychological findings. In their counseling, such persons use God's truth as revealed in Scripture as well as in scientifically determined principles of psychology and counseling. They would never negate spiritual values or principles. Yet these counselors keep Scripture and psychology separate. John Carter points out the basic epistemological assumption underlying this position: revelation can never be reduced to reason, nor can reason be reduced to revelation; God requires obedience to both reason and revelation (Carter 1977, 204).

The *integrated view* blends Scripture with psychology. Carter points out that the basic epistemological assumption here is that since God is the author of both revelation and reason, all truth is ultimately part of a unified or integrated whole (Carter 1977, 204). The integrated view stresses not only the scriptural message concerning sin and salvation, but also the cultural mandate that God has given us to replenish and master the earth. To fulfill God's mandate, we are obliged to learn all we can about His handiwork, including ourselves. The wise counselor will emphasize God's providence, sovereignty, and active relevance in all of His creation, alongside the good news of salvation.

The integrated view sees all problems as due to the universality of sin. All of human functioning (and the functioning of nature as well) has gone awry since the initial rebellion against God. Counselors holding the integrated view point out that there are some psychological problems which do not result from individual sin or from conscious sin. Although in principle all sickness—whether physical, spiritual, or emotional—is rooted in sin, one should differentiate between personal conscious sin and the inherited sinfulness that taints everything. All of us are in bondage to sin, but personal sin is not necessarily the cause of emotional difficulties.

The remainder of this book aims at working out a meaningful integration of Scripture and psychology. That such an approach is both desirable and practicable has been aptly stated by E. Stanley Jones. It is fitting to conclude our introductory chapter by quoting him at length (although we might not agree with him at every point):

> Two disciplines have arisen and are bidding to take over the thoughts and actions and motives of men. One is the Christian discipline. It undertakes to take over the minds and actions and motives of men and discipline them according to Jesus Christ and in the end make them into Christ-like personalities. The second discipline, psychiatry, has been largely, though not entirely, pagan. It undertakes to make man over in the image of his basic drives. . . . These two disciplines have been in large measure pulling in different directions. In the discipline of psychiatry the remedy is: Do what your desires demand; in the other, the Christian discipline, the remedy is: Do what Christ demands. The amazing discovery is being made that what Christ demands and what our drives demand are not at cross purposes—they coincide. Whatever Christ commands is what our desires demand. We are made for Him as the eye is made for light. So when you do His will you do your own deepest will. His will is our freedom. . . . Eventually the psychological discipline and the Christian discipline must coincide. For when psychology becomes truly psychological and Christianity becomes truly Christian, they must meet and help each other. [preface in Darling 1969, 8]

2

The Biblical Perspective

We must now examine the biblical evidence regarding the relationship between Christianity and psychology. It is to be noted first of all that Scripture designates human beings variously as soul, spirit, body, and mind. God's Word does not compartmentalize personhood, but presents a holistic view of human nature. The Christian, therefore, must be careful to view the total person as God's creation. The Book of Genesis depicts the human race as created beings subject to God's spiritual, psychological, and physical laws. The individual must always be perceived with that triad of interdependent laws in mind or else incomplete and false conclusions will result. The person must always be studied as a whole, that is, as a bio-psycho-spiritual being (see Figure 3). A change in one dimension will usually have ramifications in the other dimensions.

During the last hundred years, the church has regarded physical laws as valid and important in developing an understanding of humankind. Paradoxically, the relevance of psychological laws to the Christian life is often still denied. Advocates of a "no psychology" position (the spiritualized view) base their denial more on emotion than on careful and thorough study of biblical evidence. One popular "nouthetic" counselor claims that the disciplines of psychology and medicine do not adequately equip one to help clients deal with their problems:

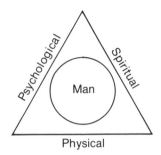

FIGURE 3   The Human Person

There is no hope in speaking of neuroses, defense mechanisms or repressions; God has not promised to do anything about such problems. But every Christian knows that Jesus came to deal with sin. Labeling sin "sin" then is kindly because it gives hope; it points to the true problem and to God's salvation. . . . Ultimately it [a psychiatric approach] constitutes rebellion against God by the rejection of His Word, His Son and His Spirit as irrelevant or inadequate. [Adams 1975, 19–20]

Other advocates of the spiritualized view say: "Sanctification, because it treats the whole man through his deepest and most profound area, his spirit, . . . is a far more powerful force than psychotherapy in dealing with mental and emotional disorders. . . . What psychotherapy attempts to heal [the old man], God already pronounced dead, null, and void" (Bobgan 1979, 149). The implication is that counseling or psychotherapy cannot be a means of sanctification.

These proponents of the spiritualized position argue for a "nothing but" approach. Only the Bible can help humans with their mental and emotional disorders; psychology is useless. But is this assumption legitimate? We will see in the rest of this chapter that the Bible itself in no way ignores psychology:

1. Psychological laws are an integral part of the creation order itself and are everywhere assumed in the Bible.
2. Throughout Scripture there is a stress on the human need for relationships.
3. The Bible is replete with data on the chief dimensions of the human personality—knowing, being, and doing.

Incorporating as much in the way of psychological data as it does, God's Word obviously does not regard psychology as useless. Rather, to deal with human needs, it integrates psychological and theological truths. If we would adopt the biblical approach, then, we too must integrate psychology and Christianity.

The Creation Order

To gain a biblical perspective on the relationship between psychology and Christianity, we must begin with the original creation when God's laws were established in the world. In creation, God caused that which was void to take on form, pattern, and law (Gen. 1:1–2). The word depicting God's creative force (*bara'*, created) is used three times in the first chapter of the Bible: "In the beginning God created the heavens and the earth" (v. 1); "So God created the great creatures of the sea and every living and moving thing with which the water teems" (v. 21); and "So God created man in his own image" (v. 27). As the formless chaos was changed into the final product of creation, God introduced multiplicity, intricacy, and order. Scientific laws are our attempt to describe the relationships and complexities we observe.

Three realms of creation can be distinguished in the three creative steps (see Figure 4):

1. The cosmos, land, vegetation (Gen. 1:1).
2. Animals, birds, sea life (Gen. 1:21).
3. Human persons (Gen. 1:27).

Various subcategories are discernible within each of these created realms. For example, in realm (1) the laws of physics, chemistry, astronomy, geology, and biology pertain. In realm (2) fall the disciplines that apply to animal life: zoology, anatomy, physiology. Realm (3) encompasses those disciplines that apply specifically to humans—sociology, logic, psychology, and theology (the message of redemption and salvation).

An important feature of the creation account in Genesis is its progression. The creation of land and vegetation precedes the creation of animals and birds. Adam and Eve, the apex of creation, were created last of all. Note that the laws of a creation category

FIGURE 4   The Stages and Laws of Creation

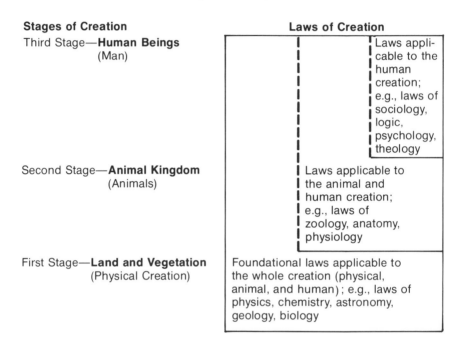

God
(The Creator)

presuppose the laws of the category(ies) beneath it. For example, the laws of psychology, which investigates the physical causes and correlates of behavior and emotions, build on and include the laws of physiology. The laws of physiology, in turn, build on and include the laws of biology and chemistry. Study of the chemistry of the body's endocrine system is therefore crucial to a complete understanding of psychology, including sexual identity and self-image as well as abnormal conditions (schizophrenia, psychosomatic illnesses, and manic-depressive psychosis).

All of God's creation categories function to form a grand whole: *the human being in God's world.* On the other hand, the three categories and their subcategories are distinct from one another. To overlook that categorical distinctiveness leads to confusion because it fails to take into account God's order of creation. For example, the laws of geology or chemistry cannot be forced into the laws of sociology. Sociology and biology apply equally to human beings, but are separate approaches. We can at least theoretically abstract a particular discipline from the whole because it is a separate category, created as such by God.

The spiritual laws which govern us are not to be equated with, but do include psychological, biological, and chemical laws. In discussing human beings, for example, the Bible everywhere assumes those physical and biological laws which are essential to the definition of human beings. Similarly, in discussing our meaning, purpose, and responses to God, the Bible assumes those laws of psychology which are essential to the definition and understanding of human personality. To study psychology, which is a God-created category, is therefore legitimate and proper, provided one remembers that it is part of a much larger whole—the spiritual laws governing humans encompass far more than psychology.

The Bible never denies the importance of the physical and biological dimension of the human person. Jesus' need for sleep and Paul's concern for Timothy's ailment (1 Tim. 5) reflect biological realities. The Old Testament prohibition against eating pork, which may carry disease-causing parasites, and the warning against touching the dead bodies of animals and humans are other examples of biblical reflection of biological realities (even though microbiological laws were not understood until the nineteenth-century discovery of the pathogenic properties of bacteria).

In like fashion, the Bible reflects psychological realities; it does not ignore psychology. In particular, it is aware of the importance of interpersonal relationships. In counseling people in mental and emotional distress, then, it is imperative to couple scriptural truths with psychology.

The Biblical Stress on Relationships

Many psychological truths are included in the biblical text. Our needs for a sense of meaning and purpose in life, for emotional growth and freedom from guilt, are underscored. Destructive emotions like anxiety, anger, guilt, and depression are discussed. Psychological concepts such as the unconscious and various defense mechanisms (repression, rationalization, denial) are acknowledged in scores of passages. Most significant is the fact that the human need for close relationships, for love and trust, is assumed throughout Scripture.

God said, "It is not good for the man to be alone" (Gen. 2:18). Adam needed human companionship and social and sexual intercourse for inner happiness and satisfaction. Eve was created to meet those needs, as he would meet hers. Note that even before the fall the social needs of the individual were singled out by God as important. After the fall not only was the need for close relationships magnified, but the relationships which remained had become severely distorted.

Figure 5 depicts the sequence described in Genesis, illustrating the importance God places on relationships. We were intended to be related to our Creator and to other human beings in a unique and fulfilling way. Through the fall Adam tainted the destiny of all who would follow him. An important result of the fall is mental and emotional suffering, formally labeled psychopathology. The dismal picture in the last phase of the figure can be restored for each of us through Christ, whose death and resurrection bring a message of healing. But there is a major obstacle keeping many non-Christians from responding to Christ: a deep-seated feeling of being unlovable. This attitude, which also results in poor interpersonal relations with other humans, is usually masked by various layers of distracting behavior by which individuals attempt to evade their real feelings about themselves.

Harry S. Sullivan, one of America's foremost psychiatrists, was well aware of the importance of good interpersonal relationships. He wrote that "personality is formed by the interpersonal relationships that an individual has, especially with close persons, during his entire lifetime. . . . Personality consists of the characteristic way a person deals with other people in his interpersonal relationships" (quoted in Chapman 1976, 69). Sullivan believed that the most intensive phase of personality development begins in infancy and extends through early adolescence. Children who have not received love and tender care will probably carry an angry and hostile attitude throughout life. Such individuals often work out their hostility in various undesirable ways.

In Romans 1, Paul picks up the theme of Genesis 3, our rebellion and fall: "The wrath of God is being revealed from heaven

FIGURE 5 The Sequence of Adam's Relationships

A. Before the Creation of Eve
God's Pronouncement: "Not Good"

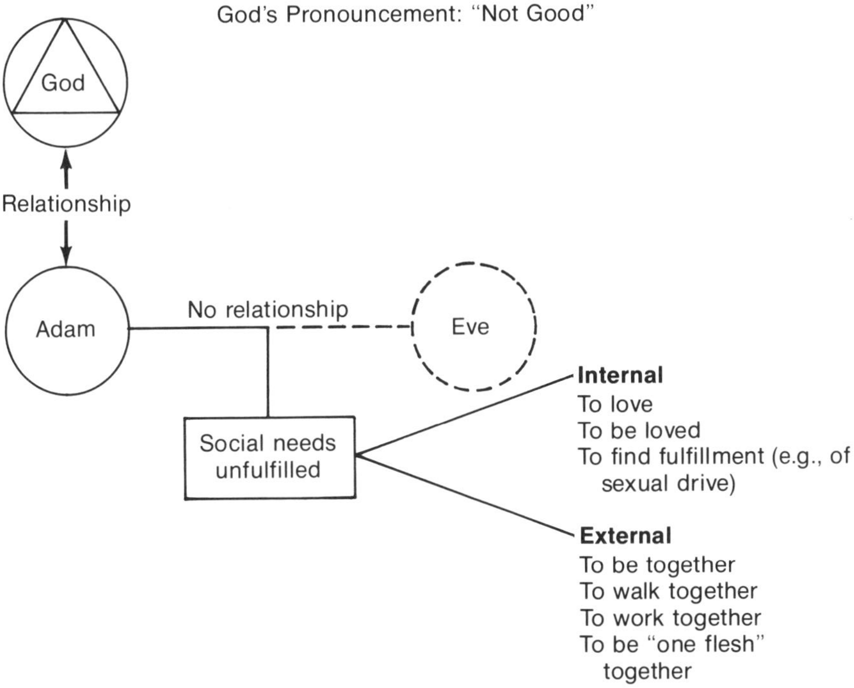
God
Relationship
Adam
No relationship
Eve
Social needs unfulfilled
Internal
To love
To be loved
To find fulfillment (e.g., of sexual drive)
External
To be together
To walk together
To work together
To be "one flesh" together

B. After the Creation of Eve
God's Pronouncement: "Good"

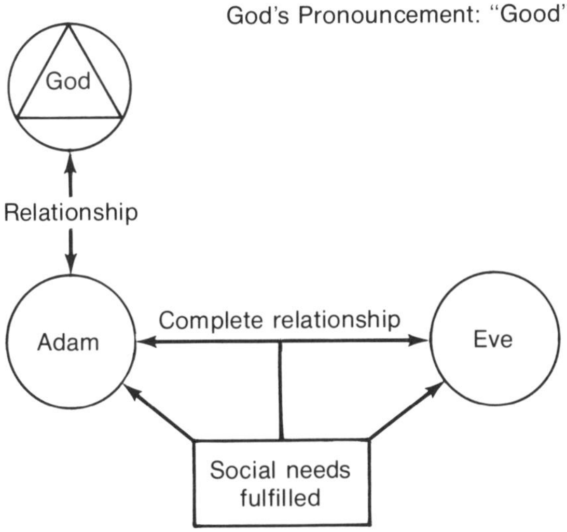
God
Relationship
Adam
Complete relationship
Eve
Social needs fulfilled

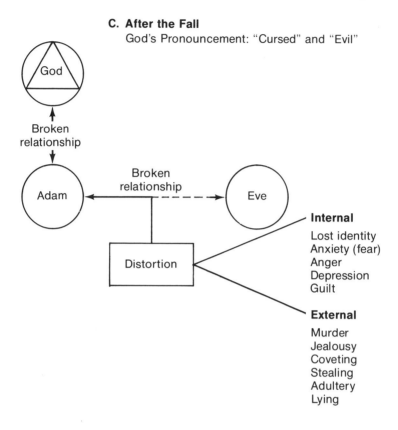

C. After the Fall
God's Pronouncement: "Cursed" and "Evil"

against all the godlessness and wickedness of men who suppress the truth by their wickedness" (Rom. 1:18). That description of the inner processes by which people deny God's existence as well as their own spiritual need reads like modern psychology. R. C. Sproul comments: "To translate Paul's analysis of man's response to the knowledge of God into contemporary categories of psychology is not a difficult task. . . . The basic states of man's reaction to God can be formulated by means of the categories of trauma, repression, and substitution" (Sproul 1974, 73–74).

A study of Paul's words and the process they describe shows that they meant for Paul exactly what we take them to mean today. Repression is a major defense mechanism, a common form of denial used by all of us. Repression is the process by which we exclude legitimate desires and impulses from our consciousness. Denied satisfaction, those desires and impulses are left to operate in the unconscious. Sproul notes that this is the very process Paul has in mind in Romans 1:18, where repression of God's truth is said to result in an ungodly lifestyle and sinful behavior.

From Genesis 2–3 and Romans 1, we can make the following observations:

1. God has created us with spiritual and social needs.
2. Good interpersonal relationships (with God and with other people) are necessary to fulfill those needs.
3. If our needs are not met by good interpersonal relationships, then, like Adam, we will tend to become spiritually, psychologically, and emotionally disoriented.

According to God's Word, every human being has intense interpersonal needs. Romans 1 shows that in their various relationships people may develop complicated and even unconscious patterns of response. Repression is one example, as is the deviant sexual behavior Paul there describes. Psychology can help us pinpoint the ways in which the fall has distorted our relationships and behavior, leaving our spiritual and social needs largely unfulfilled. Rightly applied in a Christian context, an understanding of the dynamics of repression can help suffering individuals find health and healing in their relations with God, with others, and with themselves.

To conform to the biblical teaching, we must view a human being holistically. The biblical descriptions of men and women as God's created beings assume psychological and physical laws. These essential laws affecting all levels of a person's being must be taken into account. The more of God's psychological truth we are able to discover, the more understanding we will have of great biblical truths and their application to the whole person. It is clear that psychology as a science can never instruct us concerning a human being's meaning or value, so the church must learn to distinguish between a valid psychological finding and an unwarranted (perhaps even anti-Christian) philosophical interpretation of it. If we do not make use of the valid psychological finding, we may be depriving ourselves of God's truth as revealed in psychology and thereby harm many Christian believers whose suffering could be greatly alleviated. We may also to some extent be misrepresenting God's message of redemption, for distortion of the human psyche is part of that which was redeemed by Christ's death on the cross. Christ came to heal and redeem our damaged emotions as well as our souls.

Biblical Data on the Chief Dimensions of Personality

As God's revelation to us, the Bible is the final authority for our psychospiritual life. The Bible therefore should be allowed to inform the disciplines of psychology and counseling. And, indeed, the Bible does contain a great deal of information on the human personality. In view of the many counseling theories proposed today, it is heartening that Christians can find sound biblical teaching by which to evaluate them.

In an abnormal-psychology class the distinguished professor described the human being as a thinking, feeling, and acting creature. Those three dimensions of the human being, each an important part of the whole, cover the vital functions of psychic life. All three are dealt with extensively in the Bible as well as in psychological literature. Francis Schaeffer remarks:

As God is a person, he thinks, acts and feels; so I am a person, who thinks, acts and feels. But that person is a unit. I can think of my parts in various ways: as body and spirit; or as my physical parts and my spiritual parts. I can quite correctly think of myself as intellect, will, and emotion. [Schaeffer 1971, 140]

William B. Oglesby, Jr., has refined the three categories to correspond more closely to biblical concepts—*knowing* (thinking), *being* (feeling), and *doing* (acting):

It is evident that the Bible sees all three concepts as important. Indeed, there is a sense in which the whole story of God's revelation and human response can be told in terms of "knowing," "doing," and "being." The crucial question is which of these is seen as primary and which derivative. [Oglesby 1980, 25]

In the perspective of biblical psychology, the categories of knowing, being, and doing encompass the whole of an individual, and are intertwined in such a way that they cannot really be compartmentalized. Understanding these categories is essential to a Christian counselor. Which category is primary in our personal walk with God?

Knowing

Modern theories of knowledge emphasize the importance of accumulating and understanding data, facts, and concepts. The Greeks elevated knowledge to such a lofty position that they tended to see it as an end in itself. Although this view of knowledge is significantly absent from the Bible, it can be found in the Western world and most of the Christian church. Think of the emphasis in many churches on amassing biblical facts, on rote memory of Bible verses. Further, much of the church's counseling and preaching puts primary emphasis on the intellect.

Donald M. Lake has noted that when the term *mind* (or its equivalent) is used in the Bible, it usually refers to the whole or total person:

> There is . . . a realism, particularly about the Old Testament, that does imply that *thought* and *being* are identical. . . . "As he thinketh in his heart (mind), so is he" [Prov. 23:7]. . . . It has been indicated that neither the Old Testament nor the New Testament is concerned with dissecting man into constituent parts, elements or faculties. The being of man is a united whole and his reflective or cognitive faculties are never isolated from his total being. [Lake 1975, 229]

The Bible always presents "knowing" in terms of personal relationship. In the Hebrew language, words signifying knowledge also refer to an exercise of the affections. In asking God to accompany the Israelites, Moses said, "If I have found favor in your eyes, teach me your ways so I may know you and continue to find favor with you" (Exod. 33:13). God's response followed the same lines: "I will do the very thing you have asked, because I am pleased with you and I know you by name" (v. 17). The personal aspects of "knowing" are unmistakable here.

The Old Testament represents knowledge as deriving from personal encounter with God. The Old Testament descriptions of

God and His creation are statements of faith reflecting God's actual revelation of Himself. In contrast, the Greeks' metaphysical approach to the nature of God and His creation was necessarily speculative and detached.

Commenting on the Hebrew concept of knowing, John W. Sanderson writes:

> A Christian's understanding of know and knowledge is based upon the Hebrew meaning of these words as revealed in the Old Testament. The Old Testament Israelite grew in knowledge as he listened to God's proclamations and then committed himself to live in accord with those proclamations. Knowing involved a total awareness of the living God who is present in all His creation. Every event was understood as an act of God, *and* as an act of men who acted either obediently or disobediently to the commands of God.
>
> Knowing required an effort of will to understand the significance for oneself of God's revelation to men, and the will to live in accordance with that significance. The Old Testament Israelite developed understanding of that personal significance as he listened to the God who proclaimed Himself as the Lord of the Covenant and as he lived in God's world in an obedient or disobedient response to that covenant. Personal significance was so integral a part of Hebrew knowing, that to know entailed responsibility to act. The Old Testament believer not only acquired information, but he acknowledged a personal relationship that committed him to act in accord with what he knew.
>
> The Old Testament believer was aware of what he "knew" when he lived his commitment, when he exercised his knowledge in every part of his life. . . . To know God involved loving Him: You shall love the Lord your God with all your heart and with all your soul and with all your might. [Sanderson 1972, 12–13]

The New Testament approach to knowing and knowledge is very similar. Note Jesus' prayer for His disciples just before the crucifixion: "Now this is eternal life: that they may know you, the only true God, and Jesus Christ, whom you have sent" (John 17:3).

In all four prison epistles—Ephesians, Philippians, Colossians, and Philemon—the apostle Paul begins with a prayer that the addressees might "know" what it means to be in Christ.

I keep asking that the God of our Lord Jesus Christ, the glorious Father, may give you the Spirit of wisdom and revelation, so that you may know him better. [Eph. 1:17]

And this is my prayer: that your love may abound more and more in knowledge and depth of insight. [Phil. 1:9]

For this reason, since the day we heard about you, we have not stopped praying for you and asking God to fill you with the knowledge of his will through all spiritual wisdom and understanding. [Col. 1:9]

I pray that you may be active in sharing your faith, so that you will have a full understanding [knowledge] of every good thing we have in Christ. [Philem. 6]

In each prayer Paul uses the Greek word *epignōsis*, although the usual word for knowledge in the Greek is *gnōsis*. In these four instances he adds the prefix *epi* to indicate "a full or complete knowledge of." *Epignōsis* denotes a more thorough knowledge, which Kenneth Wuest says "grasps and penetrates into an object . . . open for all to appropriate, not a secret mystery" (Wuest 1966, 1:175).

In both Testaments "knowledge" is existentially internalized and personally acted on. John Sanderson notes the continuity between the Old and New Testament concept of "knowledge":

This formative functioning of Hebrew "knowing" was not changed by New Testament revelation. Christ, God in human form, became the living embodiment to which every Christian is called to be conformed. "Knowing" now requires acknowledgment of Christ as the Son of the living God (I John 2:2, 3). It requires a personal relationship to Jesus Christ, a relationship that embodies all of life, every moment, every aspect. [Sanderson 1972, 13]

The contemporary understanding of "knowledge" is far different from these scriptural definitions. Greek philosophy has wrongly persuaded us that knowledge consists of accumulating a mass of observations and then formulating speculative theories about them. Greek knowledge was interested in the essence of things rather than in the relationship between the knower and what was observed. Knowledge of creation was pursued apart from its religious origin. Even the Greek interest in God was in

His essence, not in His relationship to the world and people He created. That kind of knowledge leads to objective talk about God rather than acknowledgment of and obedience to Him.

To summarize, the Bible does not prize the Greek and modern-day stress on intellectualism and even warns against it. The apostle Paul asked:

> Where is the wise man? Where is the scholar? Where is the philosopher of this age? . . . Jews demand miraculous signs and Greeks look for wisdom, but we preach Christ crucified: a stumbling block to Jews and foolishness to Gentiles, but to those whom God has called, both Jews and Greeks, Christ the power of God and the wisdom of God. [1 Cor. 1:20, 22–24]

The biblical view of "knowledge" stands as a restraint to those in evangelical Christianity who see the accumulation of biblical facts or comprehension of abstruse theological doctrines as sanctification.

Being

"Being" is the second vital dimension of human personality. In our study of knowing we referred to the mind. To discuss being we need to examine the biblical concept of the heart.

Johannes Behm says that heart refers to our inner essence. "The heart, the innermost part of man, represents the ego, the person. . . . Thus the heart is supremely the one centre in man to which God turns, in which the religious life is rooted, which determines moral conduct" (Behm 1965, 3:612). Owen Brandon remarks:

> Like other anthropological terms in the Old Testament, heart is also used very frequently in a psychological sense, as the center or focus in man's inner personal life. The heart is the source, or spring, of motives; the seat of the passions; the center of the thought processes; the spring of conscience. Heart, in fact, is associated with what is now meant by the cognitive, affective and volitional elements of personal life. [Brandon 1966, 262]

The Hebrew and Greek words translated "heart" are among the most important in the Bible. H. Wheeler Robinson has analyzed the various senses in which these words are used:

Sense	O.T.	N.T.
Personality	257	33
Emotional State	166	19
Intellectual Activity	204	23
Volition	195	22

[cited in Douglas 1962, 140]

Note that the number of times "heart" refers to thinking, the number of times it refers to feeling, and the number of times it refers to acting are nearly equal. The heart can thus be said to involve cognition, affect, and volition (see Figure 6). Franz Delitzsch states that the heart is the center of the psychospiritual ("pneumatico-psychical") life; this incorporates thought and conceptions, feelings and affections, will and desire (Delitzsch 1977, 293–94). These three aspects of the heart should be viewed as occurring simultaneously and mutually affecting each other. By combining Figure 6 with Figure 3, which depicts the human person as a bio-psycho-spiritual being, Figure 7 demonstrates the proper way of viewing the heart.

The Bible underlines the key role of the heart in Christian life and thought. By nature the heart is wicked and evil (Jer. 17:9). It is on the heart that God looks (1 Sam. 16:7), with the heart that we believe and are justified (Rom. 10:10), and from the heart that obedience springs (Rom. 6:17). The heart is the internal source for all of our external actions (Luke 6:45). As the center of the individual, it is the seat of emotional response and expression. The full spectrum of emotions, from joy to depression and from love to hatred, is ascribed to the heart.

Scripture regards the emotions of the heart as of great importance. Yet the place of emotions has been misunderstood by most of the evangelical Christian community. At best, emotions are merely tolerated. More often, they are treated as wrong or sinful. Indeed, much Christian theology has somehow gone awry on this key matter. Consider, for example, the impact of the Westminster Confession's statement that "there is but one only living and true God, who is . . . without body, parts, or passions."

Barry Applewhite relates the story of a seven-year-old Spartan boy who had been removed from his home to prepare for a life

FIGURE 6   The Three Aspects of the Human Heart

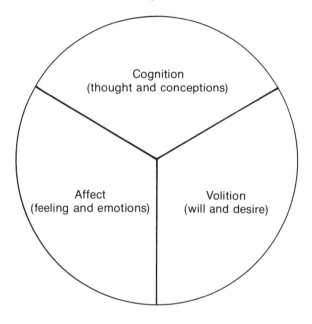

FIGURE 7   The Proper Way of Viewing the Heart

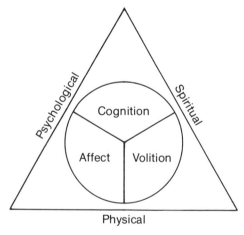

of disciplined military service. In his training he was taught to live off the land. Meeting one of his instructors on a pathway, the boy hid under his tunic a fox which he had stolen for food. Hiding all traces of emotion as he had been taught, the boy calmly kept talking while the fox gnawed savagely at his body. He fell dead without his face ever having shown any signs of emotion or pain. Applewhite notes that "many evangelical Christians would make admirable Spartans. As a group we have gone beyond the cultural standards which encourage us to hide our emotions. Covering up feeling has become an unwritten article of our Christian faith" (Applewhite 1980, 11).

According to the Bible, however, emotions and feelings have a clearly defined role in the Christian frame of reference. Basically, emotions are psychic reactions triggered by stimuli emanating from either the outside world or the inner self. As the brain is stimulated by an event (external) or thought (internal), past experiences, present circumstances, and expectations concerning the future are rapidly processed and produce an emotional response. That emotional response is essentially threefold. First there is a perceptual or cortical response. Second there is a physiological change affecting, among other things, respiration and heartbeat. Third there is the conscious feeling or sensation of the specific emotion. Figure 8 pictures the basic process of emotional response.

FIGURE 8   Emotional Response

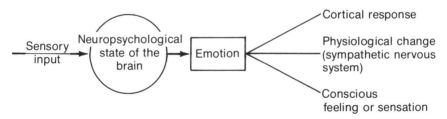

The brain is composed of a voluntary area and an involuntary area which are connected electrochemically to exchange messages. The involuntary area of the brain, called the limbic system, includes the brain stem and the midbrain. That area plays a major role in regulating feelings and emotions. It receives stimuli from the senses (touch, smell, sound, taste, and sight). It experiences in its nerve centers instinctual responses which are relayed to the voluntary or rational (cognitive) part of the brain, which is called the cortex.

Psychiatrist David Viscott has pointed out parallels between

the emotional pain sensed in the brain during psychological stress
and the sensation of physical pain:

> To understand the emotional and psychological effects of pain, it
> is helpful to understand its physical nature. Physiologically, the
> sensation of pain is transmitted through specific nerve fibers and
> is perceived where any sensory receptor is overloaded beyond its
> normal capacity to receive and transmit information. When pres-
> sure becomes too severe or temperature too hot or sound too loud,
> the stimulus is no longer perceived as pressure, temperature or
> sound, but as pain. An electrical current called the current of injury
> is initiated in the nerve ending and is sent along to the brain. The
> painful impulse produces an avoidance response that causes us to
> remove the threatened part of the body from danger—a reaction
> that often occurs automatically.
>
> This avoidance response is basic to the understanding of human
> feelings, because painful human feelings also produce a current of
> injury, telling us that we are in danger and that we must protect
> ourselves. Feelings can be overloaded just as any other system can.
> [Viscott 1976, 22–23]

The brain's role in regard to our feelings is complex. The human being is the only member of God's creation with frontal
lobes, which give us the unique ability to reason logically, to
worship, and to pray. The frontal lobes, with their capacity to
reason, are dependent on the involuntary or limbic system of the
brain, the center of our feelings. The rational part of the brain,
the cerebrum, overlies and is dependent on the lower part of the
brain, the limbic system and brain stem. The reason for belabor-
ing these physiological facts is to show that the cognitive and the
emotional or affective aspects of the brain are inextricably bound
to one another. "Facts" and "feelings" are part of the same process. The brain does not separate feelings from facts or facts from
feelings. There is little distinction between the two: all feelings
are psychological and neurological arousal attached to facts.

> There is a two-way relation between affective and cognitive proc-
> esses. The affective reaction yields information. This is an im-
> portant factor in the organization of the dispositions—habits,
> attitudes, interests, values, sentiments, etc. The cognitive process
> . . . perceptions, memories, fantasies . . . are in turn potent sources
> of feeling and emotion . . . . And in conscious awareness, the cog-
> nitive and affective components fuse. [Young 1975, 39–40]

Nor does the Bible make a distinction between facts and feelings, that is, between the cognitive and the affective. We deal not with facts *or* feelings, but with facts *and* feelings.

Consider as an illustration of the bond between fact and feeling the case of a little boy who is told by his parents that he is bad. In his frame of reference he may accept his parents' word as fact. That arouses a neurological feeling of hurt, rejection, and shame. As time passes, given continued input of parental rejection, the child may develop an overpowering feeling of being bad and worthless. In the personal mythology of the child it is both fact and feeling—an irrational perception perhaps, but also a very powerful affect. To quote Viscott once again:

> Feelings are our reaction to what we perceive and in turn they color and define our perception of the world. Feelings, in fact, are the world we live in. Because so much of what we know depends upon our feelings, to be awash in confusing or dimly perceived feelings is to be overwhelmed by a confusing world. Our feelings are our reaction to what we have perceived through our senses and they shape our reaction to what we will experience in the future. . . . I believe this suggests that the world is largely one of our own creation. . . . Understanding feelings is the key to mastery of ourselves. [Viscott 1976, 11–13]

By seeing emotions or feelings as a key aspect of the heart, we see that they are also a key part of one's being. As a key to being, they are of vital importance in the life of the Christian. Regrettably, as we stated earlier, emotions have been unjustifiably de-emphasized in the evangelical church.

The nouthetic school of counseling teaches that the "feeling-motivated life of sin oriented towards the self" is in direct opposition to the "commandment-oriented life of holiness oriented towards God" (Adams 1973, 118). According to this school of thought, living according to feelings rather than obeying God's commandments is the basic hindrance to holiness and must be dealt with by the Christian counselor. In the words of John Carter, "the real thrust of [Jay] Adams' whole approach is that listening to one's feelings is detrimental. Even having any feelings at all appears to be a liability since they are so easily directed away from God's commandments" (Carter 1975, 146). Adams himself confirms Carter's analysis. Although he states that feelings play an important and vital role in human functioning, at the same time and "with equal vigor" he emphasizes

> the unimportance of feelings. Feelings cannot be allowed to function in place of other capacities any more than the eye may be used to hear or the ear to see. . . . The Christian's guide . . . is not his feelings; it is the Bible. Any whisper to the contrary in counseling, any hint that feelings constitute an additional or even another (though lesser) guide for Christian living must be resisted. . . . While the counselee often is strongly motivated by his feelings to seek help . . . nevertheless, the Biblical solution to his problem rarely can be reached by attempting to alter his feelings. The change of feelings will take place when the change of attitude or behavior has been effected. This takes place because the counselee judges that the change of attitude or behavior is good. This judgment triggers better feelings. . . . Human beings have not been constructed in such a way that it is possible to obey a command to change feelings unaided. [Adams 1977, 23–24]

Two remarks concerning this perspective are appropriate in the light of our earlier comments on "being" and "heart." First, Adams supposes that right feelings follow right thinking and behavior. That is in sharp contrast to the biblical concept that behavior emanates from the heart (where feelings are operant). Adams's position seems to isolate feelings as a separate response instead of seeing that, according to Scripture, cognition, affect, and volition all flow and operate together. Second, actual nouthetic-counseling sessions do not deal with affect or emotions but with behavior. Bad feelings are viewed as the result of bad behavior rather than its cause. What would a nouthetic counselor do with a client suffering from an emotional disorder where the mood disturbance is clearly primary or neurochemical and the cause of the thought and behavior problems? (There is abundant evidence of cases in which the primary disorder is one of mood or feeling.) A counselor who refuses to work with a client's feelings will be of little help in such cases.

One more point needs to be made before we can leave our discussion of the heart. Since God views our heart as the central influence in the Christian life, it is imperative for us to know how it can be transformed from being "deceitful above all things" to "white as snow." How is the condition of our heart altered? No more important question can be asked in psychology—or philosophy. The biblical answer is clear. The heart is changed through a relationship with Jesus Christ. Christian theology ultimately focuses on that relationship, which is available to all who trust in Christ. According to the Bible, there is no other way in which the heart and the human person can be significantly changed. In the Old Testament, only a personal relationship with the Lord, the covenant God, could cause a life to change. David asked God to work in his heart: "Create in me a pure heart, O God, and renew a steadfast spirit within me" (Ps. 51:10); "Search me, O God, and know my heart; test me and know my anxious thoughts" (Ps. 139:23). In the Book of Ezekiel, God's role in renewing the human heart is stressed: "I will give them an undivided heart and put a new spirit in them; I will remove from them their heart of stone and give them a heart of flesh. Then they will follow my decrees and be careful to keep my laws. They will be my people, and I will be their God" (Ezek. 11:19–20). And in the New Testament, Paul emphasizes the necessity of Christ's dwelling in the heart:

> I pray that out of [the Father's] glorious riches he may strengthen you with power through his Spirit in your inner being, so that Christ may dwell in your hearts through faith. And I pray that you, being rooted and established in love, may have power, together with all the saints, to grasp how wide and long and high and deep is the love of Christ, and to know this love that surpasses knowledge—that you may be filled to the measure of all the fullness of God. [Eph. 3:16–19]

Doing

"Doing" is the third vital dimension of human personality. As the mind relates to knowing and the heart to being, so the human will relates to doing. Perhaps the most relevant biblical passage appears in the Epistle to the Romans:

> I do not understand what I do. For what I want to do I do not do, but what I hate I do. And if I do what I do not want to do, I agree that the law is good. . . . For I have the desire to do what is good,

but I cannot carry it out. For what I do is not the good I want to do; no, the evil I do not want to do—this I keep on doing. Now if I do what I do not want to do, it is no longer I who do it, but it is sin living in me that does it. . . . What a wretched man I am! Who will rescue me from this body of death? [Rom. 7:15–16, 18–20, 24]

Paul here articulates his inability to "do." That is to say, he cannot on the mere strength of his own will live a godly and righteous life. It is significant that whenever the Bible tells us to do something, it is always within the context of relationship to God. Without Him we can do nothing. Paul underscores this principle in the next chapter: "Therefore, there is now no condemnation for those who are in Christ Jesus" (Rom. 8:1). Paul was a failure when his religion rested on his own performance. But when he became one of God's adopted children ("those who are in Christ Jesus"), he could see himself as triumphant—his struggle of "doing" had ceased.

The Ten Commandments given to Moses by God are sometimes regarded as a description of a religion of human performance. It is noteworthy, however, that in context they are preceded by a statement reminding the people of Israel of their covenant with God, their relationship with Him:

Hear, O Israel, the decrees and laws I declare in your hearing today. Learn them and be sure to follow them. The LORD our God made a covenant with us at Horeb. It was not with our fathers that the LORD made this covenant, but with us, with all of us who are alive here today. The LORD spoke to you face to face out of the fire on the mountain. . . . And he said: "I am the LORD your God, who brought you out of Egypt, out of the land of slavery." [Deut. 5:1–6]

Recalling the deliverance from Egypt served as a reminder of God's covenant promises and unfailing faithfulness to His people. Not only did the giving of the commandments lead to a reestablishment of the relationship with God, but the commandments themselves are relational. The first four deal with our relationship to God, the last six with our relationship to one another. The commandments pertain to more than simple actions ("doing"); they are insightful, practical instructions in living for everyone, but especially for those who are called God's people.

They are designed to meet the needs and promote the highest good of God's covenant family.

The Sermon on the Mount is also often regarded as a checklist of "do's." Such an analysis is superficial, however, missing the pivotal role of our relationship with God. For example, "Blessed are the poor in spirit" could be restated, "Blessed are those who look to God for the fulfillment of their deepest needs and for the establishment of an intimate relationship." These teachings of Jesus must be viewed in the light of His cross and resurrection, because the lifestyle described by Jesus is impossible apart from relationship with Him: "Apart from me you can do nothing" (John 15:5).

In summary, although "doing" is stressed throughout the Bible, it is always presented in conjunction with relationship to God. It never stands alone to designate a duty or service to be performed apart from encounter with God and others.

Having examined the three vital dimensions of human personality, we must ask ourselves which is primary. It is clear from our discussion that scriptural principles focus on the heart. There is nothing more important than transformation of the heart through a personal relationship with Jesus Christ. In Scripture, then, *being* is primary. As a matter of fact, personal relationship with God is an essential component of the biblical understanding of the other two dimensions of human personality. The scriptural concept of "knowing" involves a personal relationship with what is known; knowledge derives from personal encounter with God.

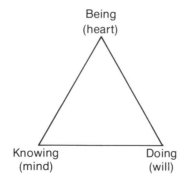

FIGURE 9   The Primacy of Being

And wherever the Bible stresses "doing," it is always within the context of relationship to God. Moreover, the three aspects of the heart do in large measure incorporate all three dimensions of the human personality: cognition (knowing), affect (being), and volition (doing). Thus, as we have indicated in Figure 9, being is the principal thrust of the biblical teaching.

3

A Proper Perspective for Today

Assessing Modern Counseling Theories

Having recognized that "being" is the principal thrust of the biblical teaching on human personality, we are now ready to establish some concrete guidelines for assessing modern counseling theories. According to Scripture, the heart can be significantly changed only by establishing and developing a personal relationship with God (and secondarily with other humans). Correspondingly, our first criterion in assessing current psychological theories will be the extent to which their preferred mode of treatment focuses on personal relationships. The second criterion will be the actual therapeutic results of each method in terms of inner growth and maturation. The third criterion will be the emphasis each theory places on the "being" of the counselor—how counselors relate to their clients is ultimately more important than what they know or do.

The Cognitive School

"Knowing," that dimension of the human personality which relates to the mind, finds a counterpart in secular therapeutic theories that stress cognition. The most prominent name in this area is, of course, Sigmund Freud. Freud's basic approach, and that used by most analysts since, is to encourage the patient both to regard the counselor as an understanding and accepting parent (transference) and to relate whatever comes to mind (free association). Through free association the counselee recalls the emotional trauma of unresolved childhood problems and faces them with the counselor. The counselor's primary task is to analyze the random thoughts and thereby teach the client about his or her fixations, conflicts, defense mechanisms (e.g., rationalization, regression, repression). By simply learning about these problem areas, the patient will get well.

Although Scripture alerts us to the fact that the human heart is often unknowable, Freud deserves credit for exploring what can be known of our unconscious selves. An examination of our dreams certainly reveals that there are unconscious forces and conflicts at work within us. The ability of hypnosis to help eyewitnesses remember details as minute as the number on a license plate is another proof of the existence of unconscious processes.

Much of God's activity in salvation and redemption takes place below the conscious level. As the Holy Spirit makes Christ real in the heart, the individual's conscious gets only partial glimpses of personal sin, righteousness, and future judgment. Francis Schaeffer likens our conscious knowledge to the tip of an iceberg: "We are constantly brought face to face with the concept of the subconscious, which is a realization that man is more than that which is on the surface. All too often the evangelical Christian acts as though there is nothing to man except that which is above the surface of the water" (Schaeffer 1971, 132).

Likewise, British psychiatrist Ernest White comments that unconscious processes play a large part in our mental life and in our conduct. Yet many Christians appear to have accepted "the conclusion that religious life is concerned only with the conscious mind." Accordingly, they have

> rejected psychological teaching lock, stock and barrel. Such an attitude is unfortunate because, insofar as truth has been discovered by psychological investigation, such people are blinding themselves to an important aspect of truth. Also they may debar themselves and others from the healing methods which are proving of such value in psychiatric treatment of nervous disorders. [White 1955, 20–21]

Although the church generally dismisses the unconscious as irrelevant or even nonexistent, counselors who see the role the unconscious plays in everyday life (in marriage, in the family, in the church) are acutely aware that it has great bearing on personal emotional and spiritual health. David, recognizing that on his own he was unable to discover true knowledge of his heart, asked God to search his thoughts (Ps. 139:23–24; the entire psalm emphasizes God's sovereignty and awareness as opposed to man's unawareness). Understanding how suppression and repression work in unconscious thought is not only helpful but needful in order to achieve wholeness. To dismiss the existence and influence of the unconscious is both unwise and unscriptural.

Another notable name in the cognitive school is Albert Ellis. In his rational-emotive therapy, Ellis makes the counselor a vigorous counterprotaganist who deliberately attacks any illogical or irrational ideas held by a disturbed client (e.g., "I must be loved by every single person in the world"). By forceful frontal attack, the therapist convinces the client that such beliefs are wrong and then helps the client to give them up.

The Humanist School

Being, that dimension of the human personality which relates to the heart, finds its counterpart in the humanist school. Carl Rogers is a primary spokesman for the humanists. The founder of client-centered (or nondirective) therapy, Rogers was the first to subject his clinical data to statistical analysis and thus bring therapy out from behind closed doors. Rogers was active as a therapist from 1930 to 1960. In his view the counselor must display three qualities to the client: empathy, positive regard, and genuineness (these will be dealt with in detail in chapter 6). Rogers's emphasis is thus on the client-counselor relationship rather than on the problem the client is facing. There are six elements present in a client-counselor relationship which achieves constructive personality change:

1. Two persons are in psychological contact.
2. The first person, whom we shall call the client, is in a state of incongruence, being vulnerable or anxious.
3. The second person, whom we shall term the therapist, is congruent or integrated in the relationship.

4. The therapist experiences unconditional positive regard for the client.
5. The therapist experiences an empathic understanding of the client's internal frame of reference and endeavors to communicate this experience to the client.
6. The communication to the client of the therapist's empathic understanding and unconditional positive regard is to a minimal degree achieved. [Ard 1966, 66]

Carl Rogers was raised in an evangelical Christian home where he made a profession of faith in Christ when he was eighteen. While attending Union Theological Seminary in New York, he abandoned his Christian position. Each of the basic elements of his therapeutic system, however, is compatible with Christian doctrine. If, as is generally believed, 85 percent of one's personality is set by the age of five or six, we may legitimately conclude that many of the basic principles of Rogerian counseling came from his Christian background.

Rogers has had great impact on the counseling field. Yet he seems to have had difficulty in going beyond his basic system of having the therapist express warm, genuine feelings and show unconditional positive regard for the client. Regrettably, that means his system is not sufficiently comprehensive to work effectively with some types of emotionally disturbed people. Even so, Carl Rogers seems to have brought a lot of God's truth to light by discovering some of God's principles for healthy human behavior.

Abraham Maslow is another important name among humanistic psychologists. He is best known for his emphasis on self-actualization and for his "hierarchy of needs." As we meet our needs on a certain level, a higher set of needs will come to dominate our lives. Our most basic needs are, of course, physiological. Food, water, sleep, sex, shelter, and oxygen are all necessary for human survival, and a deficiency in just one of those areas results in neglect of the needs on higher levels. After our physiological needs are met, "there will emerge the love and affection and belongingness needs." Then come "esteem needs," which Maslow subdivides into (1) a desire for strength, competence, and adequacy, and (2) a desire for reputation or prestige. After those needs have been met, a person can focus on self-actualization

(Maslow 1954, 43–45). Maslow identifies ten characteristics of a person who has achieved self-actualization:

1. Clearer, more efficient perception of reality.
2. More openness to experience.
3. Increased integration, wholeness and unity of the person.
4. Increased spontaneity, expressiveness; full functioning; aliveness.
5. A real self; a firm identity; autonomy, uniqueness.
6. Increased objectivity, detachment, transcendence of self.
7. Recovery of creativeness.
8. Ability to fuse concreteness and abstractness.
9. Democratic character structure.
10. Ability to love. [Maslow 1968, 157]

Obviously, both Rogers and Maslow stress a person's being. That is reminiscent of the biblical focus on the heart, the inner essence of the human personality.

The Behaviorist School

Turning to the "doing" dimension of the human personality, we come to those schools of psychotherapy that stress a person's external, observable behavior. Behaviorists generally have no concern with inner needs, drives, or psychodynamics, which are the focal points in the cognitive and humanist schools. The therapy utilized by the behaviorists is called behavior modification. It aims at removing a patient's undesirable symptoms by concentrating on directly observable manifestations of abnormality.

Drawing on the experiments of Ivan Pavlov, John Watson, the founder of behaviorism, quickly perceived the implications of the idea that conditioning is a fundamental determinant of behavior. In his famous "Little Albert" experiment, Watson was able to demonstrate that emotional reaction or response can be learned. When Little Albert (an eleven-month-old infant) heard a sudden noise, he would experience fear. On the other hand, the sight of a white rat produced no fear. When the noise and the rat were introduced together, however, he became afraid of the rat; soon the rat alone would cause him fear. Then objects resembling the rat, such as a rabbit or a fur coat, also created fear. This is an example of classical conditioning, which is at work on all of us all the time. The introduction of a specific stimulus results in an involuntary response.

Using the principles of what is termed operant conditioning, B. F. Skinner has become the leading figure in the behaviorist school. Operant conditioning differs from classical conditioning in that the therapist does not introduce a stimulus in order to evoke an involuntary response, but must wait for a desired or undesired voluntary action to occur. Then, through an elaborate system of rewards and punishments, desired behaviors are reinforced and maintained, and undesired behaviors are extinguished. Skinner has taken the basic concepts of behaviorism and honed them to razor-sharp precision. It is doubtful, however, that he is justified in claiming that all of human behavior is the product of operant conditioning (which would mean that the individual has no real freedom or dignity).

Another figure prominent in the behaviorist school is William Glasser, the founder of reality therapy. Glasser stresses the individual's current behavior and his or her responsibility for that behavior. The therapist draws the counselee's behavior into the open to be examined. "What are you doing?" is the key question. Feelings are allowed to be expressed but are not attended to, since they are considered a result of the behavior. If, after describing their behavior, counselees say that they are not happy, they are encouraged to draw up a specific plan to alter their behavior. They are given full responsibility for executing that plan; the counselor tolerates no excuses for failing to follow through. Glasser believes that alcoholism and depression are chosen behaviors; responsibility for a new plan of behavior will result in positive change.

Although Christian counselors should pay primary attention to the schools of counseling that stress inner development through personal relationships, the schools of therapy stressing the "knowing" and "doing" dimensions of personality do have contributions to make. The cognitive schools help identify and explain the problem areas (internal conflicts and negative social learnings) which need correction. The behaviorist schools help in the elimination of improper behavior and in the formation of personal relationships that will bring lasting inner change.

Most Christian schools of counseling seem to emphasize the

behaviorist approach (as do most preaching and teaching). Since the Bible is so clear in stating that *doing derives from being,* it is ironic to find the evangelical church thus directing its efforts in the direction of "doing." Jay Adams, for instance, speaks extensively of the dehabituation of "sinful behavior patterns," and, like Glasser, is interested primarily in present behavior. Feelings and social development, as well as the influence of family and environment, are for the most part considered unimportant.

But the words of Jesus have a different ring: "The good man brings good things out of the good stored up in his heart, and the evil man brings evil things out of the evil stored up in his heart. For out of the overflow of his heart his mouth speaks" (Luke 6:45). Jesus taught that the heart is the seat of behavior. It seems misguided, then, for Christian counselors to try to change a client's actions from bad to good without stressing a transformation of the heart through the establishment and development of personal relationships. That kind of counseling bypasses the heart and short-circuits the biblical process. By contrast, effective counseling emphasizes that the heart must have a dynamic relationship with God and His people. The changes thus produced will be reflected in everyday living.

The Limitations of Psychology

Now that we have briefly assessed modern counseling theories, we must determine the extent to which psychology can legitimately be utilized. The science of psychology is, of course, limited. It is limited to describing persons as they are. The findings of psychology, regardless of their thoroughness or extensiveness, can never accomplish more than to describe personality. Like any science, psychology merely observes. By definition, it cannot make a statement about the meaning of life, nor can it supply us with values, morals, goals, or proper motivations. Yet human beings are vitally interested in these matters.

Psychologists can clinically observe basic human nature, they can study brain waves in the laboratory, but they cannot speak with authority about the philosophical implications of their observations. Of course, psychologists as individuals hold all sorts of philosophical ideas. Regrettably, philosophical statements made by leaders in psychiatry and psychology have caused a large number of Christians to be skeptical of the entire scientific enterprise. For example, Freud attributed belief in God to human wishes and fears. Rogers renounced his earlier Christian beliefs. Skinner has said that human beings are biologically determined. Such statements, however, do not mean that we must discard all the findings of those schools which Freud, Rogers, and Skinner so ably represent. We simply need to recognize when they are speaking as philosophers and when they are speaking as psychologists.

The Valid Use of Psychology

Christian counselors, then, can legitimately utilize the findings of psychology. In this connection it is worth noting that, unlike many modern evangelicals, the church has on many occasions not rejected the study of the human person (psychology). The Puritans, for example, were astute physicians of the soul, and some of them were expert in dealing with mental problems, especially melancholy (what we now call depression). They were aware of the human tendency to see things as our passions represent them rather than as they really are.

The Puritans faced depression head on; that is, they did not try to spiritualize the problem when they did not understand it. Thomas Brooks said, "The cure of melancholy belongs rather to the physician than to the divine, to Galen than to Paul" (quoted in Lewis 1975, 89). The Puritan writer Christopher Love gave a concise description of melancholy: "The understanding may be darkened, the fancy troubled, reason perverted and the soul darkened" (Lewis 1975, 87). Brooks gave a lengthier description:

> Melancholy is a dark and dusky humor which disturbs both the soul and the body, and the cure of it belongs to the physical [rather] than to the divine. . . . It is a humour that unfits a man for all sorts of services, but especially those that concern his soul, his spiritual estate, his everlasting condition. The melancholic person tries the physician, grieves the minister, wounds relations and makes sport for the devil. . . . Melancholy is a disease that works strange passions, strange imaginations and strange conclusions. [Lewis 1975, 87]

And in a sermon entitled "The Cure of Melancholy and Over Much Sorrow by Faith and Physic," Richard Baxter said:

> The passions of grief and trouble do oft overthrow the sober and sound use of reason; so that a man's judgement is corrupted and perverted by it, and is not, in that case, to be trusted: as a man in raging anger, so one in fear and great trouble of mind thinks not of things as they are but as his passion represents them. About God and religion, and about his own soul and his actions, or about his friends or enemies his judgement is perverted and is usually false. [Lewis 1975, 87–88]

Archibald Alexander (1772–1851), the first professor at Princeton Theological Seminary, was a perceptive student of human behavior. His insights on counseling, especially on dealing with depression, are remarkably valid for today. In his *Thoughts on Religious Experience* (1844), Alexander wrote concerning the causes of depression:

> But physical causes are not the only ones which produce this painful state of feeling. It is often produced, in a moment, by hearing some unpleasant intelligence, or by the occurrence of some disagreeable event. . . . When religious melancholy becomes a fixed disease, it may be reckoned among the heaviest calamities to which our suffering nature is subject. It resists all argument and rejects every topic of consolation, from whatever source it may proceed. It feeds upon distress and despair and is displeased even with the suggestion or offer of relief. The mind thus affected seizes on those ideas and truths which are most awful and terrifying. Any doctrine which excludes all hope is congenial to the melancholy spirit; it seizes on such things with an unnatural avidity and will not let them go. [Alexander 1978, 35]

Alexander tells of Timothy Rogers, a London minister who lived from 1658 to 1728. Rogers was a godly, pious, and able pastor. Yet he was overtaken by a severe depression which today would probably be diagnosed as involutional depression. Rogers's depression was so acute that he "gave up all hope of the mercy of God, and believed himself to be a vessel of wrath, designed for destruction, for the praise of the glorious justice of the Almighty" (Alexander 1978, 35). Alexander describes Rogers's condition in terms that tell us the man was clinically depressed, perhaps even psychotically depressed at times. It is clear that Alexander accepts Rogers's depressed feelings as genuine and recognizes them as the cause of the spiritual problem which clouded his perceptions. Yet Alexander does not conclude that Rogers was damned, nor does he charge him with spiritual backsliding or lack of faith. Rather he sees a severe depression that needed to be understood.

Rogers's depression eventually ran its course, as do most involutional depressions. Many Christians cared for him and prayed on his behalf. After his depression lifted, Rogers became interested in ministering to others who experienced depression. As part of this effort he wrote treatises entitled *Recovery from Sickness* and *Consolation for the Afflicted*. Alexander was so impressed with the preface in Rogers's *Discourse on Trouble of Mind and the Disease of Melancholy* that he put its contents verbatim into his own *Thoughts on Religious Experience*. Those thoughts of Rogers on depression are of such high caliber that I have reproduced them in the appendix (pp. 209–14). They are the best material I have found on counseling depressed Christians.

In contrast to the writings of Rogers, Alexander, and the Puritans, a different emphasis is evident today. In *The Christian Counselor's Manual*, Jay Adams deals with depression in a chapter entitled "Helping Depressed Persons." He holds that depression is never an isolated emotion but the result of sinful mishandling of an initial problem. Sinful response to a problem such as sickness, falling behind in one's work, negligence, or guilt is the basic cause of depression:

> Depression never need result if the initial problem is met God's way. Depression is not inevitable, something that simply happens and cannot be avoided. Nor is it ever so far gone that the depression cannot be counteracted.... The hope for depressed persons, as elsewhere, lies in this: the depression is the result of the counselee's sin. If depression were some strange, unaccountable malady that has overcome him, for which he is not responsible and consequently about which he can do nothing, hope would evaporate. ... This depression is the result of the spiral of complicating factors; it is not the direct result of the initial problem. When the initial problem is mishandled, guilt and its miseries are added to the original problem. If in turn the counselee deals with these consequences sinfully, the spiral intensifies. [Adams 1973, 378]

With regard to the actual counseling of a depressed person, Adams advises:

> Thus, nouthetic counselors adhere closely to the principle enunciated in Proverbs 28:13, "He who conceals his transgressions will not prosper, but he who confesses and forsakes them will receive mercy," and confidently assure their clients that in this way they may find mercy from God. This methodology is Biblical methodology; it is therefore certain and sure. It is fitting to and grows out of the fundamental nouthetic principle that man's problems stem from sin. [Adams 1970, 125–26]

In an article entitled "A Physician Looks at Counseling: Depression," Robert Smith recommends the same approach:

> The causes of depression . . . are spiritual and are the result of sin in the counselee's life or his reaction to stresses of life. . . . The counselor's responsibility is to work back through the physical responses to the sins and guide the counselee to biblical solutions. [Smith 1977, 85]

The difference between the approach of Archibald Alexander and that of Jay Adams is that Alexander appreciated what the study of psychology can add to our understanding of the human condition and of the Christian life. Christians need a holistic perspective from which to view problems. Psychology can give us insights about ourselves and about God's influence on our lives, insights that we might not otherwise experience.

Consider the life of Charles Spurgeon. Spurgeon was frequently in the grips of massive depressions which kept him immobilized for days at a time and drove him to consider resigning his pulpit. The pain of his depression was so great that often his only comfort was to listen to his wife read to him through the night. Spurgeon fought with such depressions for many years. In the words of his biographer:

> We can sum it all up in saying that from boyhood days dreadful moods of depression repeatedly tormented Spurgeon. Every mental and spiritual labor at such times had to be carried on under protest of spirit. "The chariot wheels drag heavily," he often sighed. "Even prayer seems like labor." [Day 1955, 177]

Spurgeon would not have labeled his depressions sin; rather, he saw them as a means to reach out to others who were likewise afflicted. "I would go into the deeps a hundred times to cheer a downcast spirit, that I might know how to speak a word in season to one that is weary" (quoted in Skoglund 1979, 52).

In a sermon on the text, "Yea, though I walk through the valley of the shadow of death, I will fear no evil: for thou art with me," Spurgeon said:

> I know that wise brethren say, "You should not give way to feelings of depression." Quite right, no more we should. But we do; and perchance when *your* brain is as weary as ours you will not bear yourselves more bravely than we do. "But desponding people are very much to be blamed." I know they are, but they are also very much to be pitied; and, perhaps, if those who blame quite so furiously could once know what depression is, they would think it cruel to scatter blame where comfort is needed. There are experiences of the children of God which are full of spiritual darkness; and I am almost persuaded that those of God's servants who have been most highly favoured have, nevertheless, suffered more times of darkness than others. [Spurgeon 1880, 230–31]

William Cowper, an eighteenth-century poet and hymn writer, was hospitalized several times, attempted suicide, thought himself condemned, and did not attend church during his later years. Martin Luther, too, at times experienced deep depression: "For more than a week I was close to the gates of death and hell. I trembled in all my members. Christ was wholly lost. I was shaken by desperation and blasphemy of God" (quoted in Bainton 1963, 14). Luther's depression was on occasion so great that "he could consider suicide and feared to pick up a carving knife for fear of what he might do to himself" (Bainton 1963, 15). Those periods of depression continued until his death (1546), long after that critical moment when he came to realize the full implication of "the just shall live by faith" (c. 1513). In every case they occurred in connection with a "loss of faith that God is good and that He is good to me" (Bainton 1950, 282–83). The list could go on—John Donne, Alexander Whyte, John Henry Jowett, Andrew Bonar, Campbell Morgan—all famous preachers who suffered from lack of self-esteem, anxiety, and other emotional ailments common to humankind.

Moving to our time, we can be thankful that advances in science are providing the church with insights into the neuropsychological composition of personality. Research into the workings of the brain has revealed the correlation between various physical factors and emotional makeup. The brain has ten billion nerve calls (neurons), each with thousands of possible connections to other cells. There is, then, a virtually infinite number of different pathways through the brain. Physical disorders here can result in mental and emotional disturbance.

In addition, studies of twins and people who have been adopted suggest that at least 50 percent of human temperament and personality is genetically determined. Especially significant are research data indicating that manic-depressive psychosis and schizophrenia may be inherited. Such disorders were once thought to be strictly psychological and/or spiritual. Many Christians suffer from primary depression, which is a disturbance in brain chemistry, not in spiritual life. A chemical or primary depression can sap one's energy, disrupt eating and sleeping patterns, and cause drastic spiritual suffering. Biochemical research has led to the development of medications which, with a minimum of side effects, can help restore brain chemistry and enable individuals to lead normal or nearly normal lives again.

It is obvious, then, that Christians should be aware of the biochemical and genetic aspects of depression and psychosis. In a paper entitled "Depression: Biochemical Abnormality or Spiritual Backsliding?" psychiatrist Walter Johnson takes Jay Adams and Tim LaHaye to task for attributing depression solely to spiritual causes:

In my own psychiatric practice I have treated many patients suffering from depression, and a significant number of individuals have been people who were totally committed to the Lord and seeking to live lives of complete dedication and surrender to Him. If moody disorders were invariably and wholly caused by a condition of alienation from God, one would expect an improvement in the mental condition of such an individual as soon as he had entered into an experience of conversion or, in the case of an erring Christian, as soon as he had confessed his sin and surrendered his life completely to the Lord Jesus Christ. This, however, is not necessarily the case. . . .

I would also like to emphasize, as further evidence that problems of a spiritual nature are not the sole causes of depression, that a treatment program based upon a theoretical framework which ignores the biological and psychological factors operating in the production of depressive conditions is liable to end in disaster. In other words, if as a result of the mistaken notion that all mental illness is caused by a faulty relationship with God, spiritual therapy alone is employed to the exclusion of medical and psychological modes of treatment, the patient's emotional condition may fail to improve. He may become worse, or even be driven to an ever-deepening despair possibly terminating in suicide. This type of reasoning is not only unscientific as we have already seen, but it is also unscriptural. In the account of the healing of the man who had been blind from birth (John 9) we are told that the disciples asked the Lord Jesus the question, "Master, who did sin, this man, or his parents, that he was born blind?" Let us note carefully our Lord's reply. "Neither hath this man sinned, nor his parents: but that the works of God should be made manifest in him." In this statement our Lord clearly teaches that disease, and this includes mental illness, is not necessarily caused directly by the sin of the individual who is affected. [Johnson 1980, 24–25]

One of my own clients, a relatively new Christian whom I have been seeing twice a week for over a year and for whom I have prescribed antidepressant medication, brought me a tape of a sermon by a well-known radio preacher. I listened with a sense of anger and despair, for his message ignores the facts of biology and psychology:

> If you are having trouble and turmoil and anxiety, and you have got to go to a counselor and you have got to take pills and you have got to take drugs and you have got all kinds of problems in your life—I'll tell you what [the real cure] is—if you have righteousness in your life, if you have purity in your life, if you have holiness in your life, you will have peace in your life.

On the contrary, there is need for both Scripture and psychology. It is God's intention that we make use of all the resources available. The church should welcome new scientific discoveries relating to mental and emotional wholeness. Such findings can undo some of the disorder precipitated by the fall. The more we subdue such disorder, the more we bring persons to wholeness and, we hope, to God.

PART TWO

The Loss and Restoration of Personal Identity

4

The Loss of Personal Identity

A loved one becomes an alcoholic. A relative is sent to a mental ward. A friend commits suicide. We ask why. Is emotional distress a chance occurrence, or is there some underlying reason for it? To cope with our own emotional problems as well as with those of others, we need to understand something about the cause of such problems. The biblical picture of human creation and the subsequent fall into sin explains how mental anguish and psychological difficulties became part of our existence. Even though the Bible is not a psychology textbook, it informs us how we came to be the complicated emotional persons we are. In fact, the Bible's teachings contain in embryonic (and sometimes more fully developed) form all the valid teachings of modern behavioral science.

God's Original Design: A Strong Self-Identity

The Book of Genesis begins with the story of creation. A living, breathing human being stood majestically as the crown of God's creative acts. 'So God created man in his own image, in the image of God he created him; male and female he created them" (Gen. 1:27). Human beings stand in a unique position because they alone have been created in God's image. As a result of God's inbreathing the "breath of life" (Gen. 2:7), human beings as par-

73

takers of the divine nature (2 Peter 1:4) transcend the animal kingdom. Adam and Eve, then, were whole and fulfilled persons. They enjoyed perfect harmony within themselves and in their relationships to God, to the rest of creation, and to one another. The creation story closes with a picture of serenity: "The man and his wife were both naked, and they felt no shame" (Gen. 2:25).

Let us note Adam and Eve's mental and emotional condition before the fall. At first they had a clear sense of their own being or selfhood. To put it another way, we could say that they had a strong self-image. Self-identity is basically each person's answer to the question "Who am I?"

Our views about ourselves are molded largely by the reflective appraisals we receive from people significant in our lives. Parents, siblings, friends, and peers are all mirrors by which we receive feedback about how we are acting: those individuals constantly indicate how they feel toward us. If we receive love, praise, and affirmation, then a good self-identity or self-image usually develops. If we receive hostility or are rejected, a poor self-image often results. Like a looking glass we in turn reflect what we imagine to be the appraisals of others (Gergen 1971, 41). Their views contribute to our answer to the question "Who am I?" The impact of the appraisals of others on the formation of our self-identity will be determined by the credibility of our appraisers, their awareness of others as individuals, and the number and consistency of appraisals we receive.

Adam and Eve, of course, had the appraisal of God, whom they knew to be eminently credible. God spoke personally to them, giving them responsibility over creation (Gen. 1:26–29). God blessed Adam and Eve, and by pronouncing all that He had made "very good," He affirmed them. The interpersonal relationship which the first two human beings had with God defined their selfhood.

Beyond reflective appraisals, there are other components that go into the development of a positive self-identity. First, an individual today must be close to someone of the same sex who is well adjusted and also perceived as an authority. Ideally this will be the individual's parent. Their relationship should be open and genuine, so the younger person can interact with the authority figure in such a way that knowledge, respect, and love ensue ("I want to be like you"). As that type of relationship grows, the younger person will take as his or her own (i.e., internalize) the values, goals, ideas, and behavior of the authority figure. "Through an incorporation of another human being and his values we are influenced in our behavior by that person and act as though we were directed by that person with his entire sense of experience" (Gaylin 1976, 95).

Consider the case, typical of many others, of a committed Christian woman in her early thirties who underwent the painful experience of divorce after her husband had left her. During her first interview with a professional counselor she complained of depression, social withdrawal, and obesity. It soon became evident that those problems resulted from her lack of a positive self-image. Her mother was still suffocating her with negative remarks about her personality and performance. Unable to separate from her mother sufficiently to establish her own ego boundaries, the daughter developed negative attitudes about herself. She could not make sufficient distinction between herself and her mother to say, "I am myself and she is herself." The result was that, depending on her mother and others to give her nurturing security, she felt depressed and tended to withdraw whenever that security was missing. Whenever relationships with others failed to provide a sense of being nurtured, feelings of weakness, helplessness, and self-hatred ruled her life.

A healthy concept of self is basic to the development of a strong sense of identity. The Greek word for self is *ego* ("I"). An example is found in Paul's words as he looked back over his life: "For I am already being poured out like a drink offering, and the time has come for my departure. I have fought the good fight, I have finished the race, I have kept the faith" (2 Tim. 4:6–7). Paul used the word *ego* to refer to his whole personhood. It was his "self" that had fought the battle and run the race and guarded the truth.

Jesus also used the term *ego* to refer to Himself. In teaching the Jews, He said, "I tell you the truth . . . before Abraham was born, I am!" (John 8:58). The words Jesus used to identify His personhood were carefully chosen. They show that He regarded Himself as the Lord of the Old Testament, who had identified Himself to Moses as "I am who I am" (cf. Exod. 3:13–15). To the question "Who am I?" a person with a positive self-identity is able to respond, "I am I. I am who I am."

Another requirement for establishing a strong sense of self-identity is a frame of reference through which the self and the world can be accurately viewed. The particular framework within which Adam and Eve had been created enabled them to see God, the world, and themselves perfectly. For they had been created in the image of God. Their world was such that they were capable of perfect attitudes, ideas, actions, and feelings. They lived in a framework of absolute truth. By virtue of their having been created in the image of God, God was their reference point in everything. From their first moments of consciousness Adam and Eve were able to view life and the world from God's perspective. Externally, God's presence was evident. Internally, God's image ruled and ordered their thoughts and feelings. The result was a totally secure self-image, which is possible only when one's identity is totally in God.

Implications of Creation in the Image of God

That Adam and Eve's frame of reference was rooted in God's truth meant that they had an absolute knowledge of *reality*. As a result, they were able to formulate ideas and develop attitudes that were thoroughly sound (see Figure 10).

"Everyone receives sensory data in a unique way so that it is not 'raw' data but data filtered and interpreted by the receiver" (Felker 1974, 3). It is probable that Adam and Eve, unlike us, received all types of sensory input perfectly from their Edenic environment (which included the presence of God). As Adam and Eve received data from their world (through the senses of seeing, hearing, touching, tasting, and smelling) and experienced relationship with God and with one another, they were able to formulate ideas that were completely valid, including self-perceptions. They were able to give true appraisals of themselves as God's special creation. They knew their place in the world. Unlike us, they did not worry about being unable to understand themselves or wonder why they thought, felt, and acted as they did. They felt no need to distort reality by denying, suppressing, or repressing it. The confused ideas and mental problems which result from such distortion were absent from their experience.

Just as absolute knowledge of reality enabled Adam and Eve to

FIGURE 10   The Two Perceptual Frameworks of Adam and Eve

A. The Image of God—
   Absolute Truth
   (before fall)

B. The Human Ego—
   Assumptive Truth
   (after fall)

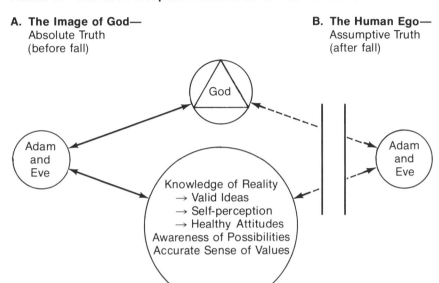

formulate valid ideas, it enabled them to manifest healthy attitudes. Attitudes are the emotions or feelings that one has toward someone or something. We are told that Adam and Eve "felt no shame" (Gen. 2:25). Shame is brought on by realization that one has not lived up to certain standards or ideals. Often it involves feeling inferior, inadequate, or evil. Shame and guilt inevitably undermine our self-esteem and often result in anxiety and depression. But Adam and Eve experienced none of that.

Moreover, it is likely that Adam and Eve had absolute knowledge not only of what things actually were (reality) but of what they could be (*possibilities*). Of course, Adam and Eve, because of their sinless state, were unaware of many things we know. They did not know evil, or what the loss of the image of God and absolute truth would involve. They did not know all the results of disobedience and rebellion. "You will certainly die," God had said in warning them about the forbidden tree, but they did not know all that death would entail.

In addition, Adam and Eve likely had an accurate sense of *values*, that is, of how things should be. They knew the joy of fellowship with the Lord. They knew love, honesty, and genuineness from experiencing those qualities in their life with God and with one another. They knew that obedience was the only condition for becoming all that God intended.

The Loss of a Positive Self-Identity

In spite of their creation in the image of God, Adam and Eve wanted to become equal with God, and so they ate fruit from the tree of the knowledge of good and evil. Suddenly and catastrophically, the image of God in humankind was shattered. That was the beginning of mental anguish and psychological struggle. Confusion and distortion now marked the human sense of personal identity. The tragedy of existence in a fallen state had begun. ·Adam and Eve no longer viewed themselves and the rest of creation through the framework of the image of God, but through the framework of their own egos. Let me explain what I mean.

Adam and Eve lost their sense of self because they rebelled against God. They were no longer united with God in fellowship and love. God's image in them was defiled, although it still existed. God expelled them from His presence, and so they lost God as their reference point. They had to look to themselves for some kind of integration. Their own egos became the axis around which their thinking, feelings, and actions revolved. Their identity, no longer God-centered, became self-centered. The human being instead of God became their standard of truth. Such truth is only assumptive at best, not absolute.

What are the implications of the fact that Adam and Eve now viewed everything from within the framework of their own egos? When operating from within the framework of the image of God, they had possessed an absolute knowledge of reality. But now Adam and Eve's egos filtered and censored external reality in order to avoid pain. When Adam said, "I was afraid because I was naked" (Gen. 3:10), he really meant, "I am afraid of you, Lord." He was expressing his fear of the truth (the personal presence of God) that previously had made him feel secure and loved. To Adam reality was no longer the presence of God but something of a vacuum. Confused, disoriented, and panicky, he had become the prototype of many of the mental disorders confronting us individually and collectively today.

Adam remembered that God had said that he and Eve would surely die if they disobeyed. Now Adam feared God's reality so much that he hid from it. Though describing modern humanity, Ronald Laing has given us a vivid picture of the thoughts and feelings which must have prompted Adam when he attempted to hide from God:

> The individual [Adam] feels that, like the vacuum, he is empty. But this emptiness is him. Although in other ways he longs for the emptiness to be filled, he dreads the possibility of this happening because he has come to feel that all he can be is the awful nothingness of just this very vacuum. Any "contact" with reality is then in itself experienced as a dreadful threat because reality as experienced from this position is necessarily implosive and thus . . . in itself a threat to what identity the individual [Adam] is able to suppose himself to have. [Laing 1965, 45–46]

Putting ourselves in Adam's place, we see that he feared God's punishment. Before, Adam had been given life and enriched by God; now he feared that God's influence on him would be impoverishing and deadening. Adam was afraid that God might make him into an object with no being, no life. Fear of nonbeing has long been a major problem. Paul Tillich spoke of the anxiety of nonbeing; Jean-Paul Sartre also spoke of it in *Being and Nothingness,* describing life as nausea.

After the fall Adam and Eve's perceptions changed. No longer did they have an absolute knowledge of reality; their vision of reality was blurred (see Figure 10). The distortion was both external (what they saw) and internal (how they felt); it encompassed everything. Hence they were no longer able to formulate ideas that were completely valid. Before, they saw fully; now they saw only partially. Seeing things fully brings understanding. Seeing in part brings partial understanding at best and, more often, misunderstanding. The apostle Paul spoke of "seeing through a glass darkly."

Since Adam and Eve's ideas were distorted, their self-perceptions were likewise distorted. As they filtered sensory data from their environment, they came to regard themselves negatively (they covered their nakedness). Adam now viewed Eve negatively (Gen. 3:12—"the woman you put here with me—she gave me some fruit from the tree"). Their self-concept was no longer secure. In panic they fled from the reality of God's presence. They could no longer think the way they had before. They were no longer sure about what to do, where to go, or whom to love.

Some of the most serious psychological problems today involve similar disorders. Mental institutions continually work with people who regard themselves as Christ, Napoleon, or some other prominent historical figure. But to a lesser degree all of us have mistaken ideas about who we are. Because of the fall no one has a totally true picture of himself or herself.

Just as the loss of absolute knowledge of reality prevented Adam and Eve from formulating valid ideas (including self-concepts), it also prevented them from maintaining healthy attitudes and feelings. Their behavior revealed their guilt and shame. They had gone their autonomous way. They would now experience anxiety and depression. They had died, spiritually and emotionally.

Moreover, Adam and Eve lost their absolute knowledge not only of reality, but of possibilities (what might be) as well. Not knowing what to expect left them fearful about the future. Their bright prospects were extinguished. Unless God somehow helped them, they could never again have a sense of security.

Finally, Adam and Eve lost their accurate sense of values. "Right" had meant refraining from eating the fruit of the tree of the knowledge of good and evil. When they disobeyed, they acquired a knowledge of evil. They became aware of the difference between good and evil. Worse still, they were aligned with evil. Realization that they had violated the standard of right gave them a sense of shame and guilt.

Today, as descendants of Adam and Eve, we live in a world of changing values. The relativism of modern culture has its roots right here in Genesis. If we are to have absolute values, they will have to come from outside ourselves.

What is the basic distinguishing mark between the two frameworks within which Adam and Eve viewed God and the world (i.e., the framework of the image of God [absolute truth] and the framework of the human ego [assumptive truth])? The answer lies in the crucial concept of relationship. Adam and Eve's creation in the image of God set them apart from the animals and gave them special qualities (such as morality and love) that they might be in intimate relationship with God and with one another.

> Central to the idea [that God made man in His own image] is an understanding of man in a warm and intimate relationship with God, a relationship so special that no other creature shares this precious bond. It is not too much to call it a Father-son relationship which like all relationships needs constant fellowship and open contact if it is going to mature into loving, responsive, and permanent association between God and man. Man is not actually named God's child in the Genesis narratives, but what is there implicitly is worked out explicitly in the rest of the biblical revelation. So the "image" designates the potential of man called to share the warmth of fellowship and life with Him. [Carey 1977, 39–40]

The Bible speaks of covenants, commandments, doctrines, sins, and holiness. All of these concepts imply some sort of relationship—a vertical relationship between God and humans, a horizontal relationship between humans, or perhaps both. Yet these concepts are often discussed as if they were entities unto themselves, as if they had nothing to do with relationships. To discuss these concepts apart from the relationships which they involve results in false and damaging teaching. When we interpret Scripture, a central hermeneutical question should be: "What relationship(s) is (are) involved here? How should this passage be interpreted in light of that relationship (those relationships)?" Because relationships were partially lost, and certainly blurred, in the fall, we can easily lose sight of their critical role in both theology and psychology.

When Adam and Eve fell, they lost their harmonious relationship with God, with the rest of creation, with one another, and even with their real selves. The word *loss* is central to an understanding of what happened. When Adam told God that he hid because he was afraid, he was saying in essence, "I have lost God, so I no longer belong. I am afraid and insecure." He was also saying, "I have lost perfection, so I no longer feel a sense of self-esteem. Instead I feel guilty and ashamed." God asked Adam, "Who told you that you were naked?" Of course, no one had. God was accentuating the fact that the shame Adam felt was self-caused. Adam had brought it on himself, and he was feeling its consequences. Finally, Adam was saying, "I have lost control, so I am weak and feel depressed." Before the fall, Adam was God's foreman, commissioned to subdue the earth and able to live in happiness without fear. He was strong enough to deal satisfactorily with any situation that might come his way (that meant he was strong enough even to resist the desire to be as God, the desire to be autonomous). Now he no longer had that strength. He undoubtedly felt inferior and insignificant.

FIGURE 11   What Adam Lost When He Fell

Specific Loss	Personal Consequence	Corresponding Emotion
God	Loss of sense of belonging	Anxiety, insecurity
Perfection	Loss of self-esteem	Guilt, shame
Control	Loss of strength	Depression, feeling of helplessness

Figure 11 depicts the dire consequences of Adam's broken relationship with God, consequences still sorely experienced today. While tracing particular emotional problems to specific events in a client's background, the Christian counselor realizes that the ultimate cause is the loss of relationship with God. The specific events in the client's background merely exacerbated and magnified that fundamental problem.

In the right-hand column of Figure 11 we see the emergence of various emotions which are ultimately destructive to relationships, both with others and with oneself. Alongside anxiety, guilt, and depression we must include anger. We see anger already in Genesis 3. In anger Adam projected onto God the blame for what he had done ("the woman *you* put here with me—she gave me some fruit from the tree"). Then in chapter 4 we read that when God rejected Cain's offering but accepted Abel's, Cain was angry. Clinically, anger and depression often go together. And, as a matter of fact, the Bible does tell us that Cain was depressed as well as angry:

Then the LORD said to Cain, "Why are you angry? Why is your
face downcast? If you do what is right, will you not be accepted?
But if you do not do what is right, sin is crouching at your door;
it desires to have you, but you must master it." [Gen. 4:6–7]

God's question, "Why is your face downcast [literally, fallen]?"
clearly implies that Cain was depressed. For in a number of an-
cient languages an expression like "his face fell" was widely used
to denote depression or sadness. It has recently been contended
that in Genesis 4:6 the phrase clearly indicates depression rather
than anger: "The Lord's rejection of Cain's offering meant to Cain
... the loss of his love-object. Cain's being rejected by his love-
object results in a loss of self-esteem which is a primary characteristic of depression" (Gruber 1980, 35–36). It is noteworthy
that God does not call Cain's anger or depression sin, but warns
him that in his depressed state he is very susceptible to sin—it
is crouching at the door.

The counterbalance to all of the destructive emotions from
which we suffer as a result of the fall—anxiety and fear (Gen.
3:8–10), shame and guilt (Gen. 2:25; 3:7), depression and anger
(Gen. 4:6)—is, of course, love. Love is the means of reestablishing
broken relationships and a sense of security.

The Divided Self

Another way of viewing the consequences of the fall is to note
that Adam has lost the unity within the core of his personality.
He is now divided: the self (ego) is fractured into two negative
parts: a needing self and a rejected self. Each has powerful and
dynamic influence on the fallen personality.

The needing self is that part of Adam and of us that realizes
we have great inner needs, needs which remain unfulfilled outside a relationship with our Creator. Adam no doubt thought back
often to the days when he had fully experienced love, contentment, and perfection, which he now experienced only partially
at best. That we have inner needs crying out for fulfillment is the
key to understanding the history of redemption. Redemptive history is the whole sweep of God's seeking man to fill his needs.
When God asked Adam, "Where are you?" He was aware of the

great need which Adam was experiencing. When God in His grace promised the coming Messiah (Gen. 3:15), He was promising Adam that his deepest needs would be fulfilled. Each subsequent covenant is a promise of grace concerning the eventual satisfaction of our needs. The culmination is the new covenant in Christ. God's search for man reached its climax when the One who came to seek and to save those who are lost died at Calvary in order to restore our broken relationships along with the love, affection, and affirmation which Adam and Eve had experienced in Eden.

The rejected self is that part of our inner personality which experiences the withdrawal of love and of nurture, the severance of relations, and perhaps even abandonment by others. The etiology of the rejected self is to be found in the fall. In Genesis 3:23–24 we read: "So the LORD God banished him from the Garden of Eden to work the ground from which he had been taken. After he drove the man out, he placed on the east side of the Garden of Eden cherubim and a flaming sword." Here we have two references to God's banishment of Adam from His presence as he had intimately known it in Eden. The Hebrew phrase translated "drove the man out" (v. 24) employs a very strong word connoting rejection and alienation.

The overwhelming negative power of the rejected self can be seen in Adam's behavior. His needing self would naturally have been drawn to God, the source of love, affection, and affirmation. But the rejected self prevented him from going to the One who created and loved him. Instead Adam fled from Him who alone could have fulfilled his needs. One would have expected Adam to go to God, admit his wrong, and beg for forgiveness and restoration. But Adam fled, as he admitted, out of fear and guilt or shame. Inwardly he must have been saying, "God is angry at me; I no longer deserve Him. I'm worthless, I'm bad; I hate myself. No good person would want me now." Rejected by God, Adam condemned himself. We might say, then, that his rejected self became a rejecting self as well.

Unfortunately flight from God under the overriding power of the rejected/rejecting self leads to devastating emotional results both for Adam and for us. We are dead in our sins. Our hostility toward God and His laws is documented through all of Scripture (see especially Rom. 3:10–18). In the formation of the rejected/rejecting self we have the core of what is variously called the principle of sin, the sinful nature, the flesh. Its psychological manifestations are extremely negative (see Rom. 1:28–32; Gal. 5:19–21).

The ultimate conclusion of the needing self's alienation from God and consequent lack of fulfillment is hell. In hell none of the deficiencies of the needing self will be filled. In addition, the anxiety and fears clustered around the rejected self will be horribly realized in God's total abandonment. By contrast, Christians can experience fulfillment. The deficiencies of the needing self are filled when we become God's adopted children, when we can cry, "*Abba,* Father" (Rom. 8:15–17). And the fears of the rejected self can be laid to rest because for those in Christ there is no condemnation nor separation from His love (Rom. 8:1, 39).

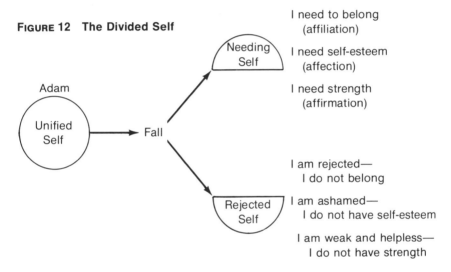

FIGURE 12   The Divided Self

I need to belong
(affiliation)

Needing Self

I need self-esteem
(affection)

I need strength
(affirmation)

Adam

Unified Self → Fall

I am rejected—
I do not belong

Rejected Self

I am ashamed—
I do not have self-esteem

I am weak and helpless—
I do not have strength

Figure 12 depicts the divided self. How the problems presented by the divided self can be clinically worked out will be explored in chapters 6–8. Suffice it to say here that the image of the divided self helps us to understand the message of the Bible regarding the needs of emotionally fallen man and God's activity in the redemptive process. By understanding these matters we will be better able to relate and apply the message of redemption.

The Emergence of Sin

With the fall, sin emerged into the world. The word *sin* first occurs in the account of God's rejection of Cain's sacrifice (Gen.

4:7—"if you do not do what is right, sin is crouching at your door"). Sin must always be viewed in the context of a broken relationship with God. The word *sin* is never used in the Bible as an isolated entity, that is, merely as a label depicting a particular state of heart or mind, or a particular type of behavior. Whenever the word occurs in the Bible, it alerts human beings to the fact that their relationship with God is insufficiently intimate. Louis Berkhof defines sin as "essentially a breaking away from God, opposition to God, and transgression of the law of God. Sin should always be defined in terms of man's relation to God and to his will as expressed in the moral laws" (Berkhof 1963, 230–31).

The word the apostle Paul chose to use in referring to Adam's fall is most instructive in this connection: "For if the many died by the trespass of the one man, how much more did God's grace and the gift that came by the grace of the one man, Jesus Christ, overflow to the many!" (Rom. 5:15). The word *trespass (paraptōma)* comes from the noun *ptōma,* which means "fall" or "collapse," and the prefix *para,* which means "at, by, or near the side of." The literal meaning of *paraptōma* is, then, "a falling near the side of." The picture suggested is that as God and Adam were walking together, Adam suddenly fell away. Paul is clearly suggesting that the essence of Adam's fall was his deliberate breaking of his intimate relationship with God.

All too often when we use the word *sin,* we are not thinking in terms of our broken relationship with God. What does it mean to tell someone that he or she is a sinner? Sometimes the word is used as a label or as a method to control or criticize people, rather than to lead them to a closer relationship with God. It is used with little concern for the needs of others. But the apostle Paul seldom used the word as an isolated reprimand. Rather, he usually pointed at some specific unacceptable behavior and indicated that it was incompatible with a relationship with Christ.

Sin has played an immense role in human lives since the fall. We all sin and are responsible for the *willful* aspect of our sinful actions. It should be noted, however, that in some cases we are also sinned against and on that account find ourselves vulnerable to sin.

Consider the example of a homosexual man who becomes a Christian. If his is a classic case, some rather definite factors in his past caused his lust for other men. Is he responsible for his homosexual orientation, a condition which he did not desire but which resulted from faulty upbringing? No, his desiring other men is not necessarily a sin. But the Bible is clear that if he acts out his homosexual orientation and has sexual relations with other men, he is violating God's created order ("male and female created he them"). Such activity will hinder his relationship with God. Responsibility for his faulty orientation may, in all likelihood, be laid at the doorstep of others. He, however, must take responsibility for his sexual actions.

One man, after becoming a Christian, came to me for counseling because of his homosexual orientation. Although he was in his thirties, he had never had erotic thoughts or fantasies about women. His sexual experiences had been limited to younger men. He had been reared by an older mother who overprotected him. He slept with her until he was nine. His father, who was bad-tempered and also older than the norm, rejected the boy, continually subjecting him to abuse and ridicule. Sexual seduction by an older male cousin increased the homosexual orientation. My client came to depend on younger males to gratify his need for power ("I am not totally weak"), acceptance, and self-esteem. Now he had not asked for the environment in which he was reared or for his homosexual impulses. He was sinned against by those who created his disordered sexual orientation. His personal sin was the acting out of his impulses with other males. Although he stopped such behavior after he became a Christian, his sexual orientation stayed with him. (Some Christian psychologists are finding that certain homosexuals, when motivated by Christian convictions and thoroughly committed to a therapy program, are able to change their orientation to heterosexual.)

Having noted that there is a crucial difference between a faulty orientation and an actual carrying out of that orientation, we must at this point also draw a distinction between original sin and what psychologist Curry Mavis calls "maladaptive impulses," both of which are results of the fall. When Adam fell, genuine needs were born. The need to belong, the need for self-esteem, and the need for control are now the most prominent driving forces of personality. Do we meet our needs in the positive ways God has designed, thus producing happiness and fulfillment? Or do we try to meet our needs in our own way, which ultimately leads to self-destruction? We would like to think that we try to meet our needs in God's way. Yet history and our individual experience usually demonstrate the opposite. Like Adam, we choose to go our own way. Mavis notes two inner forces which incline us to wrongdoing as we attempt to meet our needs: "First, there are the natural and inborn tendencies which theologians have termed original or innate sin. Second, there are repressed complexes and maladaptive impulses which have been acquired in life experiences" (Mavis 1963, 60).

According to the Bible, it is our natural disposition to be at enmity with God. Paul told the Romans, "The mind of sinful man is death . . . because the sinful mind is hostile to God. It does not submit to God's law, nor can it do so" (Rom. 8:6–7). In discussing original sin the Westminster Confession (6.4) states that "from this original corruption, whereby we are all utterly indisposed, disabled, and made opposite to all good, and wholly inclined to all evil, do proceed all actual transgressions."

Maladaptive impulses are qualitatively different from natural (original) sin. We all have legitimate needs and legitimate impulses to meet those needs. We also have a tendency toward sinful ways. Maladaptive impulses seek the normal and right ends of life (meeting needs), but by the wrong means.

Our backgrounds have taught all of us sinful patterns of meeting needs. No home, school, or church environment is free from psychological forces that have a negative influence on the development of children and in later life eventuate in ungodly tendencies as they seek to meet their needs. For example, the person who receives little affirmation and approval from parents may, in an effort to achieve self-esteem and a sense of worth, develop a tendency to work too hard, exaggerate the facts, or compromise biblical standards.

Because the world is basically sinful, we all have attitudes, complexes, or maladaptive drives that incline us to meet our needs in our own ways rather than God's. Christians should realize that these acquired psychic reactions make us resistant to the will of God and, therefore, need to be dealt with. Mavis provides a word of caution, however:

Many advocates of the deeper spiritual life have invalidated their message by claiming too much. They have failed to discriminate between the innate sinful impulses (original sin) and the acquired tendencies that originated in unfavorable life experiences. They have overlooked the fact that tendencies to wrongdoing may spring even from a sanctified life. With an attitude of overgeneralization, they have failed to see that emotionally toned ideas become drives to action; that repressed experiences provide motivation in behavior; and that traumatic experiences remain dynamic after they have been forgotten. Many ardent advocates for the deeper spiritual life have forgotten that truth is obscured by overstatement as well as understatement.

The sincere person on the Christian quest becomes confused and disillusioned when he/she fails to recognize that the Holy Spirit does not cleanse away, like a great divine psychiatrist, all the emotional complexes, defense mechanisms, anxieties, and other ineffective psychological processes when He fills the human heart with His sanctifying presence. Paul recognized that many of the psychic processes remain in the heart after the filling of the Spirit. After describing personal freedom from the law of sin and death in Romans 8, he says, "Likewise the Spirit also helpeth our infirmities" (Romans 8:26). The Holy Spirit employs a different kind of divine therapy in resolving the acquired tendencies to wrongdoing. He does not remove all of them by an act of cleansing, but rather He helps believers to gain insight into their maladjustments and to resolve them by His strengthening presence. [Mavis 1963, 62–63]

FIGURE 13   Degeneration–Regeneration–Sanctification

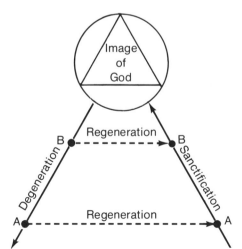

Figure 13 illustrates what Mavis is saying. We are created in the image of God, but because of the fall we are born in a state of degeneration. As long as we are outside a saving relationship with Jesus Christ, our basic nature remains fallen. After exercising faith in Christ, we are reborn and then re-created by the Holy Spirit (regenerated) in order that the image of God may be revealed in us. Becoming a Christian (regeneration) moves a person from the process of degeneration to the process of sanctification.

It should be emphasized, however, that initially a person moves from one process to the other at the same point. For example, Person A becomes a Christian but, because of environmental forces, starts at a lower level in the process of sanctification than does Person B, who is better adjusted emotionally. Person A is regenerated but in psychological adjustment still stands considerably below Person B. However, both A and B have acquired the dynamic of the Holy Spirit, which will give them positive insight into themselves and result in personality change. Accordingly, both should expect to see significant psychospiritual growth.

Further Results of the Fall

Physical Problems

God warned Adam and Eve that if they disobeyed, they would surely die. The death to which they were condemned affects all aspects of human functioning—spiritual, psychological, and physical. Because of the fall, humans suffer from bodily disorders, deformities, abnormalities, and deterioration. Indeed, all physical illness is a result of Adam's fall and the subsequent decay of the body. This includes not only cardiovascular disease and crippled limbs, but also all the physical problems that are related to emotional suffering.

Recent research regarding the brain indicates that many psychological problems involve a physical component, and in some cases this component is the primary cause. Certain types of depression, which occur for no apparent psychological reason, may result from poor synaptic responses between the brain's neurons. Such a chemical imbalance, from a biblical perspective, can be directly traced to the fall's deteriorating effect on our bodies. Therefore, the use of antidepressant medications to correct the defect is legitimate, since they help to bring about the redemption that Christ Himself will complete in the future.

The Ineffectiveness of the Will

Much Christian counseling, especially counseling that emphasizes the "doing" dimension of the human personality, claims that therapeutic change is merely "a matter of the will." A person can determine to change his behavior, to give up certain compulsions, or even not to feel a certain way. Jay Adams advises depressed people to change their sinful behavior patterns: "Go ahead and do it. . . . *No matter how you feel.* Ask God to help you" (Adams 1973, 379). That advice takes too mild a view of the fall and its effects on human functioning. The will, along with the cognitive and affective aspects of the heart, has been badly damaged; to a large extent human beings no longer have control over themselves.

According to theologian Cornelius Van Til:

> The Bible plainly teaches that what we are determines what we do. But we are here concerned to point out that in the case of original man his instincts did not hamper his freedom. We might be tempted to express this idea by saying that before the fall man's will controlled his subconscious life, while after the fall man's subconscious life controlled his will. This we believe is largely true. . . .
>
> Hence we can more fully and more definitely distinguish man as he was originally from man as he became after the fall, by saying that before the fall the *will* of man, insofar as it was controlled by his instincts, was not therewith hindered in the least in the freedom of its action, while after the fall the will of man, insofar as it is controlled by his instincts, is practically a slave of those instincts. Before the fall both man's instincts and his will in the narrower sense of the term, that is, insofar as it acts self-consciously, were good, while after the fall both the instincts and the will, in the narrower sense of the term, became evil. [Van Til 1947, 48–49]

There is very little that can be accomplished by the will of fallen humanity. The Bible is clear that before we experience salvation, the only thing we can do to please God is to will to be in proper relationship with Christ. Jesus said, "Apart from me you can do nothing" (John 15:5). That also holds true for us after salvation. We cannot simply by an act of our will change ourselves into what God wants us to be. That requires the empowering of the Holy Spirit. In fact, the strength of the self-centered ego is so tremendous that our will to do God's will can be nearly immobilized (Rom. 7:15ff.). Paul chided those Galatians who had been persuaded by the Judaizers that the Christian life is largely a matter of human works and willpower: "Did you receive the Spirit by observing the law, or by believing what you heard? Are you so foolish? After beginning with the Spirit, are you now trying to attain your goal [King James: are ye now made perfect] by human effort?" (Gal. 3:2–3). We must depend not on our will, but on the Holy Spirit. And as we continue to depend on Him, our will will be strengthened so that we can more consistently meet God's requirements for godly living—and psychological health.

5

The Restoration of Personal Identity

The Bible is frequently concerned with the matter of identity: the identity of God, the identity of the people of Israel, the identity of the early church, our new identity in Christ. James A. Sanders notes that the Bible

> is not primarily a source book for the history of Israel . . . and the early church . . . but rather a mirror for the identity of the believing community [and its individuals] which in any era turns to ask who it is and what it is to do. . . . The believing community abuses the Bible whenever it seeks in it models for its morality, but reads it with validity when it finds in the Bible mirrors for its identity. [Sanders 1972, xv–xvi]

In the previous chapter we saw that when Adam and Eve fell, they lost their sense of identity. But God had a plan to restore it. The Scriptures unfold this plan of redemption, which culminates in the death and resurrection of Jesus Christ. God's search for man, His means of restoring human identity, begins with His question to Adam, "Where are you?" and climaxes at the cross with Christ's atonement for our rebellion. Jesus gave back to us our sense of identity by taking the punishment, rejection, and shame that we deserve. Through a response of faith to the person and work of Christ on the cross, human beings are able to recover their lost identity. If there is no such response of faith, any attempt to recover human identity will prove futile. As Francis Schaeffer says,

> The non-Christian psychologist, by the very nature of what he believes, will try to bring about an integration on the level of the original rebellion. He cannot go beyond that. As a result, the integration will be an attempt to relate what is broken in the person to the animals and the machines or it will ask for a romantic leap. [Schaeffer 1971, 129]

God's firm sense of self (the Old Testament "I am who I am") is also seen in Jesus' sense of identity—"Before Abraham was born, I am!" Through personal relationship with Christ by faith, Christians can begin to experience a similar positive self-concept ("I am I; I am who I am"). As their relationship with Christ deepens through the indwelling of the Holy Spirit, their self-image will grow even stronger.

The Parable of the Loving Father

God's design for our finding our true identity is poignantly symbolized in the parable of the prodigal son, which is found in Luke 15:11–32. This parable, which for our purposes might better be called the parable of the loving father, merits careful study.

> There was a man who had two sons. The younger one said to his father, "Father, give me my share of the estate." So he divided his property between them. [Luke 15:11–12]

The first character drawing our attention is the younger son, who came to his father to ask for his inheritance, which would have been one-third of the estate (the firstborn received a double share—Deut. 21:17). The son's request betrayed what must have been his private thoughts: "I wish Father were dead so I could have my inheritance *now*." The son wanted to leave home, and he did.

> Not long after that, the younger son got together all he had, set off for a distant country and there squandered his wealth in wild living. After he had spent everything, there was a severe famine in

that whole country, and he began to be in need. So he went and hired himself out to a citizen of that country, who sent him to his fields to feed pigs. He longed to fill his stomach with the pods that the pigs were eating, but no one gave him anything. [Luke 15:13–16]

The younger son, who represents the tax collectors and sinners with whom Jesus was dining, had said in essence, "I cannot find my identity here with my father. I must go out into the world to find out who I really am." His search for himself ended in failure, for when famine struck the distant country, he found himself bankrupt and deserted by friends. Eventually he was hired to feed pigs. In being forced to feed unclean animals (Lev. 11:7)—and in the employ of a Gentile at that—not only did he not find his true self, but he also lost his ethnic identity as a Jew. He slowly began to realize that apart from a proper relationship with his father any attempt to find himself would be futile.

The elder son, who represents the Pharisees and the teachers of the law who were standing by as Jesus told the parable, does not appear until the end of the story. He was working in the fields, no doubt as his father's right-hand man, when the younger brother arrived home from his calamitous misadventures in the distant land. A feast of welcome was well under way when the older son returned from work.

Meanwhile, the older son was in the field. When he came near the house, he heard music and dancing. So he called one of the servants and asked him what was going on. "Your brother has come," he replied, "and your father has killed the fattened calf because he has him back safe and sound." [Luke 15:25–27]

The older brother reacted in anger against what he viewed as an unmerited celebration. He apparently was annoyed at his brother's quick and easy acceptance back into the home.

The older brother became angry and refused to go in. So his father went out and pleaded with him. But he answered his father, "Look! All these years I've been slaving for you and never disobeyed your orders. Yet you never gave me even a young goat so I could celebrate with my friends. But when this son of yours who has squandered your property with prostitutes comes home, you kill the fattened calf for him!" [Luke 15:28–30]

Here we gain some insight into the identity quest of the older brother. His protest that he had never broken a single command of his father shows that he thought he could find his identity through his own performance. His goal was to be a dutiful, achieving son. He thought worth consisted in works. Like his prodigal brother, he did not understand that his true self could be found only in a proper relationship with his father.

The older son was angry that his brother had been accepted on the sole basis of their father's love and grace (free, unmerited favor). He was so upset that he would not even go into the house and, when the father attempted to bring the two sons together,

FIGURE 14   The Restoration of Human Identity—The Proper Perspective

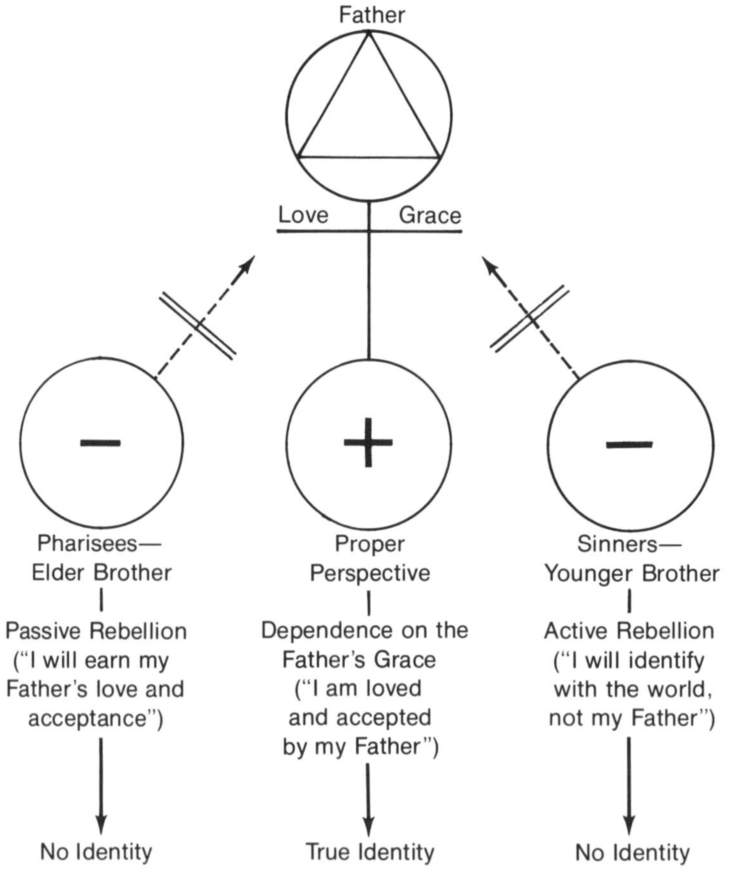

Pharisees— Elder Brother	Proper Perspective	Sinners— Younger Brother
Passive Rebellion ("I will earn my Father's love and acceptance")	Dependence on the Father's Grace ("I am loved and accepted by my Father")	Active Rebellion ("I will identify with the world, not my Father")
No Identity	True Identity	No Identity

referred to his brother as "this son of yours." That the father responded to his wayward son with gracious love, but had made no such response to his dutiful son's efforts to find self-identity through works was beyond the older brother's comprehension. He even rubbed in the fact that his rebellious brother had squandered his inheritance on prostitutes. The older son simply did not understand that finding his true identity depended on the unmerited favor of his father, not on his own works.

The occasion of this parable was the anger and dismay of the Pharisees (the older brother) that Jesus would stoop to eat with sinners (the younger brother). "But the Pharisees and the teachers of the law muttered, 'This man welcomes sinners and eats with them' " (Luke 15:2). In telling the story of the loving father Jesus was saying in effect that neither the Pharisees nor the sinners had a proper perspective. Neither group understood the heart of God the Father; neither group knew the path to restoration of human identity. Sinners try to find themselves through association with the world; Pharisees try to achieve a positive self-image through their own works. Jesus pointed out by contrast that the only means of restoring human identity is the love and grace of God the Father toward the persons He has created (see Figure 14).

> But while he [the younger son] was still a long way off, his father saw him and was filled with compassion for him; he ran to his son, threw his arms around him and kissed him. [Luke 15:20]

The picture is graphic. Having heard that his son was coming, the father humiliated himself by running out to meet him (the Greek word actually means "he raced"), undignified behavior for a man of his age and position.

> But now the father races down the road. To do so, he must take the front edge of his robes in his hand like a teenager. When he does this, his undergarments show. All of this is frightfully shameful for him. The gang in the street will be distracted from tormenting the prodigal. Instead they will run after the father, amazed at seeing this old man shaming himself publicly. It is the very "compassion" mentioned in the text that leads the father to race out to his son. He knows what his son will face in the village. He takes upon himself the shame and humiliation due the prodigal. [Bailey 1973, 54–55]

Notice that the father accepted the son as he was—unconditionally. Father embraced son in spite of all the marks of rebellion still on him: tattered clothes, disheveled appearance, gaunt body, and drawn face, as well as the sweat of travel—and smell of pigs. That quality of love and grace defies human comprehension. The young son felt totally unworthy of such acceptance:

> "Father, I have sinned against heaven and against you. I am no longer worthy to be called your son." [Luke 15:21]

Even though the son had seen his father running toward him and had been engulfed with his embraces and kisses, he felt so uncomfortable that he tried to push his father away. The father cut off the speech the son had probably rehearsed. It was the father's turn to dictate the terms of their relationship.

> But the father said to his servants, "Quick! Bring the best robe and put it on him. Put a ring on his finger and sandals on his feet. Bring the fattened calf and kill it. Let's have a feast and celebrate. For this son of mine was dead and is alive again; he was lost and is found." [Luke 15:22–24]

The ring (probably a signet ring bearing the family mark) and the best clothing indicate that the father had taken the son back into the family. The son had been considered dead, but now he was alive. In effect, the father was adopting a new son.

Jesus is teaching us that by returning to Him we can find our true identity. We miss the meaning of life if we act like either brother in the parable. Jesus accepts us unconditionally, no matter where we may have sought our identity before coming home to Him.

"In Christ"—The Identity of the Christian

The New Testament defines the believer as someone who is "in Christ (Jesus)." That phrase occurs more than a hundred times in the Epistles. To identify oneself properly, one might say, "I am _____ in Christ Jesus." John Stott notes that to be "in Christ" does not mean to be locked up or to live inside Christ; rather, it means to be united with Him in a close, personal way:

Let me clarify immediately that our ... preposition "in" when used in relation to Christ, is not used spatially. To be "in" Christ does not mean to be "inside" Christ, as the family are in the house when they spend an evening together, or as clothes are kept in a cupboard or tools in a box. No, to be "in" Christ is not to be located inside him or to be locked up in him for safety, but rather to be united to him in a very close personal relationship. ... The Good News Bible is quite correct to render the words "in Christ" by the expression "in union with Christ." [Stott 1979, 52]

Sin and temptation are threats to our identity, challenges to who we are "in Christ." By sinning, we push ourselves away from our relationship with Christ and His church. We temporarily renounce who we are—just like the prodigal. When Satan attacks us, he begins by trying to destroy our identity in Christ. In this connection it is significant that when Satan tempted Jesus in the wilderness, he began by attacking His identity as well: "If you are the Son of God . . ." (Luke 4:1–12).

God's commandments are designed to help us strengthen our identity in Christ and thus ward off Satan. They should never be thought of apart from our relationship with Christ. The law, the Ten Commandments, and the Sermon on the Mount serve as guidelines to help us fully realize our identity as Christians.

The Bible has a name for God's teaching on how we should live: the name is law, in Hebrew, torah. The biblical idea of God's law is not in the first instance that of a public legal code (though God gave Israel its public legal code), but of friendly authoritative instruction such as a wise father gives his children. That is what torah means. God's law is his kindly word to us as our creator who cares for us and wants to lead us into rewarding paths. To be sure, disobedience to God's law will bring retribution, but the law was given not primarily to threaten us, rather to guide us into what is good for us. ... God's revealed law stands related to us human beings as the owner's manual stands related to our cars. You need not read the manual, or take any notice of what it says— but you can expect your car to give you trouble if you handle it differently from the way the manual directs. And we can expect our human nature, which was designed to operate in obedience to God's law and experience freedom and fulfillment, contentment and joy in so doing, to give a vast amount of trouble if we break

the bounds and use or rather misuse our humanity in a different
way. [Packer 1978, 24–26]

If we think of God's commands as guidelines to foster our
identity in Christ, they can be a wonderful aid in counseling
Christians. That Paul regarded them in this way is evident from
his letters. He often began his letters by noting a particular point
of difficulty in the church to which he was writing. Then he
presented a lengthy discourse on the person of Jesus Christ, reminding the people in the church that they were *in Christ.* The
idea of being in Christ is the fundamental thought expressed on
every page of Paul's letters. As an apostle of the resurrected and
living Christ, Paul wanted his readers to experience union with
Him. Only after he had reminded the Christians of their position
in Christ did he suggest specific behavior patterns for them to
adopt. Only after emphasizing the believers' identity in Christ
did he point out that obedience to His commandments would
enable them to walk worthy of Him. That is the proper counseling sequence.

All aspects of Christian doctrine should be viewed in the context of our relationship with God. I become uncomfortable, then,
when the biblical commandments are thought of as entities totally
apart from our identity in Christ; that is, when they are regarded
as laws ordered by a god who lies in wait with a big stick for
anyone who happens to make a mistake. We must ever keep in
mind that God's commandments do not exist apart from their
Giver, who initiated a loving relationship with His people before
He established laws. Commandments do not exist in a vacuum,
nor have they been given because they happen to prescribe the
way God feels we should act. Rather, behind them lie our deepest
needs. Each of God's commandments is intensely personal instruction as to how we can meet one of our most vital human
needs (e.g., a sense of belonging, affection, strength). Obeying
them serves to enhance our relationship with God and sense of
self-identity in Christ.

God's Method of Restoring Human Identity—
The Three Theological Virtues

There is a unique and ingenious pattern to the process by which
God restores human identity (see Figure 15). We noted in the

previous chapter that the fall left Adam and Eve with three basic needs—a sense of belonging, affection, strength. God restores our identity by meeting those basic human needs. Each of them is fulfilled primarily by a specific member of the Trinity working personally in the individual heart. The result in each case is the development of one of the three theological virtues—faith, love, or hope. These virtues, which, as Paul mentions, endure beyond death and history, are the chief marks of the fulfilled Christian life. As God's children we should seek to please Him by cultivating them.

Faith

A basic definition of faith would include the concepts of trusting in, clinging to, relying on. The writer of Hebrews summarizes faith as "being sure of what we hope for and certain of what we do not see" (11:1). Faith has as its object someone or something that is firm, reliable, and steadfast. In the Bible faith usually means trust in the person of Christ. Jesus said, "Do not let your hearts be troubled. Trust in God; trust also in me" (John 14:1). He established Himself as the object of faith for the Christian.

Although deep spiritual faith is ultimately a gift from God, its seed can be found in the infant's implicit trust in its mother. The womb is in effect a promise to the baby that it will be cared for, and that promise is usually confirmed in early childhood. Children whose parents are faithful to that promise will find it easier to trust the promises of God in later life.

The Need to Belong

The roots of faith are to be found in the basic feeling that one belongs; lack of faith can be traced to the belief that one does not belong. Belongingness is an awareness that one is an important part of something. Basic trust is cultivated by the feeling that one is part of others and able to rely on them. We all strive to be part of a group and to experience affection. When that need is unmet, the pangs of loneliness and rejection are strong.

Much attention has been focused on the importance of touching infants if they are to develop a sense of belonging. Several studies done early in this century showed a mortality rate of nearly 100 percent for institutionalized infants who had been

FIGURE 15   The Restoration of Human Identity—The Process

Inner Need of Fallen Humanity	Sense of belonging	Affection	Strength
Personality Dimension	Knowing	Being	Doing
Component to Be Restored	Self-image (cognitive part of identity)	Self-esteem (emotional part of identity)	Self-control (volitional part of identity)
Member of the Trinity	Father	Son	Holy Spirit
Resultant Virtue	Faith	Love	Hope

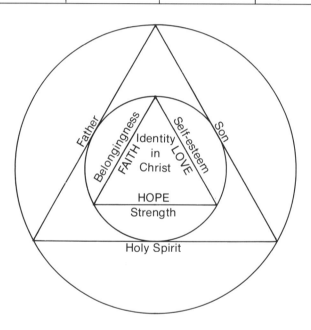

deprived of nurturing touch. Babies without a strong sense of belonging will suffer irreversible psychological damage as they go through stages of protest, despair, and eventual detachment (Burns 1980, 164). Anthropologist Ashley Montagu adds that

there is now good evidence which leads us to believe that not only does a baby want to be loved, but also that it wants to love, that all of its drives are oriented in the direction of receiving and giving love, and that if it doesn't receive love it is unable to give it—as a child or as an adult. [quoted in Goble 1970, 49]

The adult need to belong is as strong as that of an infant, although it is expressed differently. That Adam hid from God indicates that Eden had ceased to be a peaceful home for him and that he no longer felt at one with God. Adam no longer belonged. "With his disobedience, fear had entered his heart, and with it distrust" (Tournier 1968, 39). We are like Adam in that there is no place where we belong and no one with whom we feel at home.

Because of our loneliness and anxiety resulting from separation and alienation from ourselves, each other, and God, we want someone with whom we can be at one, who can be at one with us, and through whom we may find at-oneness with all. This is the deepest want of all, and the fact of our need is not at all dependent upon our being aware of it. All of us are moved by this desire whether we know it or not, and in one way or another we are seeking such a one, many of us in the wrong ways. . . . In relation to this need for at-oneness is the Gospel good news. God gave Himself in Jesus of Nazareth as the Personal Answer to man's need. [Howe 1953, 15]

The Need Met in the Father

The need to belong is met primarily in God the Father through adoption. God adopts us into His family so that we belong to Him in a special way. There are two pertinent scriptural passages:

Yet to all who received him, to those who believed in his name, he gave the right to become children of God—children born not of natural descent, nor of human decision or a husband's will, but born of God. [John 1:12–13]

For you did not receive a spirit that makes you a slave again to fear, but you received the Spirit of sonship. And by him we cry, "Abba, Father." The Spirit himself testifies with our spirit that we are God's children. [Rom. 8:15–16]

Abba is an intimate word meaning "Dear Daddy" or "Dear Papa." Being God's children implies that we receive the kind of welcome the prodigal son received when he returned home and found that he did belong after all. Adoption presupposes pardon and acceptance, and results in close relationship. "How great is the love the Father has lavished on us, that we should be called children of God!" (1 John 3:1). Our relationship with God can be far more than that between ruler and subject or between master and servant. Jesus said, "I no longer call you servants, because a servant does not know his master's business. Instead, I have called you friends" (John 15:15). A still closer, more endearing relationship exists as a consequence of adoption: "So you are no longer a slave, but a son; and since you are a son, God has made you also an heir" (Gal. 4:7).

If a child has been well cared for, and the proper attachments and bondings have been allowed to form, trust will naturally develop. On the other hand, if deprived of or rejected by a parent, a child will be kept from experiencing a sense of security and trust. The amount of trust developed in childhood usually carries over into adult life and is reflected in one's relationship to God. Someone who has experienced little or no trust in family and social relationships will find it rather difficult to exercise faith in God. But someone who has a firm trust in others will, upon realization that he or she has been adopted by God the Father, also have a strong faith in Him.

Love

The Bible calls love the greatest virtue (1 Cor. 13:13). The word used by Paul is *agapē*, which refers to a love standing above all others. *Erōs* refers to physical love. *Philia* refers to the warmth, closeness, and affection experienced in a deep friendship. *Agapē* is the supreme love of God shown in Christ when He died for the ungodly. It means, among other things, meeting another person's needs even if your own needs are not being met. It is a love that reaches beyond the normal limits, even to the point of seeking the highest good of one's enemies.

The highest form of love is possible only as we allow God to live through us. It is a fruit of the Spirit, a quality which can be produced only by God. Christians are called to be like God in demonstrating this love to others.

Agape has to do with the mind: it is not simply an emotion which rises unbidden in our hearts; it is a principle by which we deliberately live. Agape has supremely to do with the will. It is a conquest, a victory, and achievement. No one ever naturally loved his enemies. To love one's enemies is a conquest of all our natural inclinations and emotions. [Barclay 1974, 21]

Love brings emotional intimacy, with the exchange of our most personal thoughts and feelings. Sharing private thoughts and feelings with a trusted friend leads to a special kind of warmth. Harry Stack Sullivan observed that relationships of this type first occur between the ages of eight-and-a-half and ten, when a youngster normally becomes a chum of a particular member of the same sex. During that period the individual moves beyond egocentric constriction to looking to the needs (happiness, support, and feelings of worth) of the chum. Such a relationship permits validation of all the components of one's personal worth.

The Need for Self-Esteem

Love fulfills our basic need for self-esteem. Self-esteem like self-image is one of the basic components of human identity. A positive self-image and self-esteem both come ultimately from an underlying sense that one is of worth and value. Of course, the standards of worth and value will vary sharply; while one individual focuses on biblical criteria, another judges on the basis of secular criteria (e.g., physical attractiveness, wealth). Self-image is the cognitive component of identity, an intellectual knowledge of who one is: "I am a child of God; I am in Christ." Self-esteem is the emotional component of identity. A person without sufficient self-esteem might say: "Though intellectually I know who I am, I don't really feel like God's child. How could anyone love me? Even I don't love me." The emotional component is stronger than the cognitive. How we feel about ourselves is the driving force behind many of our thoughts and actions. (Remember our conclusion that being is the most important dimension of the human personality.)

There is no value judgment more important to man—no factor more decisive in his psychological development and motivation—than the estimate he passes on himself. . . . This estimate is or-

dinarily experienced by him, not (primarily) in the form of a conscious, verbalized judgment, but in the form of a feeling, a feeling
that can be hard to isolate and identify because he experiences it
constantly: it is part of every other feeling, it is involved in his
every emotional response. An emotion is the product of an evaluation; it reflects an appraisal of the beneficial or harmful relationship of some aspect of reality to oneself. Thus, a man's view
of himself is necessarily implicit in all his value-responses. Any
judgment entailing the issue, "Is this for me or against me?"—
entails a view of the "me" involved. [Branden 1976, 64–65]

We all have a need for self-respect and for the esteem of others.
That need manifests itself in two basic ways: (1) desire for
achievement and competence, and (2) desire for reputation and
prestige. Satisfaction of the need for self-esteem leads to feelings
of worth and usefulness to others. Failure to meet that need produces feelings of inferiority and helplessness. Such negative feelings produce discouragement at the least and compensatory or
neurotic trends at worst (Maslow 1954, 45).

Young people are highly susceptible to negative feelings about
themselves. A study of church youth found their number one cry
to be "the cry of self-hatred." "Distress over personal faults (self-
criticism) and the lack of self-confidence (personal anxiety) undermine feelings of self-regard. As self-criticism and anxiety
mount, self-regard drops lower and lower" (Strommen 1974, 14).
The lower our self-esteem, the more we tend to hate ourselves.

By contrast, the more love we experience, the greater will be
our self-esteem ("I am of value because I am loved"). "The small
child loses self-esteem when he loses love and attains it when he
regains love" (Fenichel 1945, 41). When love is not shown, when
we are rejected, there are serious consequences for our self-
esteem. Rejection can be overt or covert. Overt rejection is obvious. Parents, for example, may not demonstrate affection for a
child (or at least not enough to offset their displays of frustration
and anger). Covert rejection usually takes place below the conscious level of both parent and child; occasionally, however, the
child senses what is actually happening. A surface attitude of
care and concern masks a lack of true warmth and affection.

Having generally failed to follow the example of Christ, the
Western world is not characterized by giving, loving, and sharing,
but rather is materialistically oriented. The Christian values of

love and care for others have not prevailed. Instead, personal security and affluence are the main objectives of twentieth-century society. That accounts for much of the covert rejection occurring in homes today. Children are deemed less valuable than physical attractiveness, wealth, and education. Rejected by their parents, they fall into a cycle which is very difficult to break (see Figure 16).

Among the byproducts of the vicious spiral which occurs when affection and intimacy are absent are various undesirable emotions. If the need for love goes unfulfilled, a sense of shame often results ("I'm unlovable and worthless"). Frustration develops. If unabated, frustration turns to self-hate and anger. Although the anger may be unconscious, it will nonetheless be present. In some cases the anger may turn to rage, even fury. The result may be a lifestyle preoccupied with gaining power and control. The individual who is obsessed in this way will treat others ruthlessly in order to gain a sense of self-worth, release the anger pent up from past rejections, and avoid further emotional hurt.

The Need Met in the Son

Our need for self-esteem is met in the gospel. Christians have a strong basis for self-esteem in the unconditional love, acceptance, and positive regard for them which Christ demonstrated in dying on the cross. In His atoning death, Christ looked at us sinners and said, "I love you as you are." He attached no conditions to His acceptance of us except our faith. It is as if Christ had said, "You are of such worth and value to me that I am going to die, even experience hell, so that you might be adopted as my brothers and sisters."

The astonishing truth is that Jesus sees to the core of each of us and declares us of infinite worth. No part of our heart escapes His sight or His sanctifying power (to sanctify means to set apart or make holy). His love is all-inclusive; it accepts the whole of each of us.

This is momentous knowledge. There is unspeakable comfort—the sort of comfort that energizes, be it said, not evaporates—in knowing that God is constantly taking knowledge of me in love, and watching over me for my good. There is tremendous relief in knowing that His love to me is utterly realistic, based at every point on prior knowledge of the worst about me, so that no dis-

FIGURE 16   **The Cycle of Self-Esteem** (based on a figure in Norman H. Wright, *Living with Your Emotions* [Irvine, Calif.: Harvest House, 1979], p. 9)

A. General Cycle

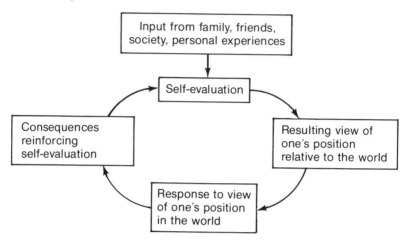

B. Cycle of Rejection

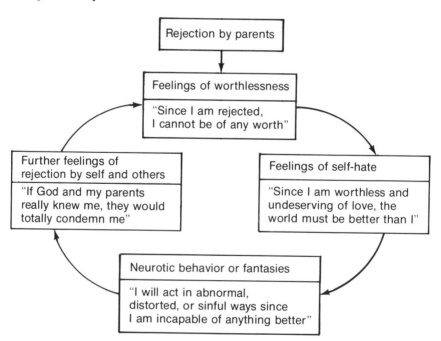

covery now can disillusion Him about me, in the way I am so often disillusioned about myself, and quench His determination to bless me. There is, certainly, great cause for humility in the thought that He sees all the twisted things about me that my fellow men do not see (and am I glad), and that He sees more corruption in me than that which I see in myself (which, in all conscience, is enough). There is, however, equally great incentive to worship and love God in the thought that for some unfathomable reason, He wants me as His friend, and desires to be my friend, and has given His Son to die for me in order to realize this purpose. [Packer 1973, 37]

Hope

The Greek word for hope, *elpis*, signifies an optimism not only toward life and its problems, but also with respect to death. The Christian hope is based on the resurrection of Jesus Christ from the dead. The apostle Peter wrote, "Praise be to the God and Father of our Lord Jesus Christ! . . . he has given us new birth into a living hope through the resurrection of Jesus Christ from the dead" (1 Peter 1:3).

As a result of the hope we have because of the resurrection, we should be characterized by an overall mood of expectation. The Christian is expectant, pushing on toward one grand and climactic goal:

Dear friends, now we are children of God, and what we will be has not yet been made known. But we know that when he appears, we shall be like him, for we shall see him as he is. Everyone who has this hope in him purifies himself, just as he is pure. [1 John 3:2–3]

As Christians, our ultimate hope is that when we see Jesus Christ face to face, we will become like Him. In anticipating that moment, we purify ourselves. The process of striving toward the goal changes us radically in that we become more holy or Christlike in our behavior. Such a life has meaning and purpose.

The Need for Control

The hope which we have because of the resurrection gives us assurance that the sense of control which Adam lost in the fall will be restored. We tend to think that who we are is determined by what we control. Having a sense of control over one's personal life and destiny is essential to any kind of proper emotional functioning. If we have a persistent feeling that life is impossible or out of control, we will be anxious and helpless. We were created with a need to exercise some degree of control over ourselves and our world. To fulfill this need requires a certain measure of strength and competence. Most important is a sense of initiative in regard to ourselves and our environment along with a reasonable assurance of a satisfactory outcome. Without initiative and a sense of being in control, we will be unable to act.

A sense that one is out of control, helpless, and unable to take any initiative in life usually results in depression ("I can't do anything right"). The feeling of helplessness (the opposite of self-control) can have a devastating effect. Many people become emotionally incapacitated out of a belief that because they were unable to accomplish something in the past, they will be unable to accomplish anything in the future ("I am trapped; I have no control over the situation or myself"). Of course, most people experience such feelings at times; but with some this becomes a way of life, an obsession which causes them to move away from others and retreat to a safe place alone.

The Need Met Through the Holy Spirit

One of the activities which God works in the heart of Christians is the restoration of their ability to exercise self-control and thereby also to exercise a measure of control over their world. Day by day the Holy Spirit builds self-control into the Christian. Self-control is a fruit of the Spirit (Gal. 5:22–23). "God did not give us a spirit of timidity, but a spirit of power, of love and of self-discipline" (2 Tim. 1:7). Strength, power, and love emanate from self-control. We do not have in mind here the overcontrol which characterizes Christians who attempt to restrain their sinful nature by repressive rules, laws, and rituals; rather, we have in mind the liberty which Christians have to give order to their lives by personally walking with Christ and living for Him daily.

As we focus on the hope of the resurrection, we recover the strength and sense of control which Adam lost. This work of the Holy Spirit, coupled with both the self-esteem which we gain as we come to realize the Son's infinite love for us and the sense of belonging, trust, and faith which we receive from the Father's adoption of us as His children, serves to restore human identity.

The Healing of the Divided Self

We saw in the preceding chapter that with the fall Adam's personality was divided into two negative parts: a needing self and a rejected self. As God's redemptive work in Christ restores human identity, it will necessarily heal the divided self as well.

Jesus points to the needing self in the first of the Beatitudes: "Blessed are the poor in spirit, for theirs is the kingdom of heaven" (Matt. 5:3). The Greek word translated "poor" is *ptōchos*, which suggests someone who crouches or cowers in fear, and in particular, a beggar well aware of his wretched condition. The "poor in spirit," then, are like beggars who, having no resources in themselves, outstretch their hands to heaven. Their needs can be met only through a relationship with God.

In John 6:35, as Jesus addresses the crowds whom He had miraculously fed the preceding day, He gives specific teaching as to how the inner needs occasioned by the fall can be satisfied: "I am the bread of life. He who comes to me will never go hungry, and he who believes in me will never be thirsty." In this verse Jesus uses the basic need for food and water to symbolize much deeper spiritual needs, needs which can be fulfilled only by a personal relationship with Him and His Father. Jesus is in essence saying that all needs are met in Him. He is the Bread of Life; the hungry, thirsty person (the needing self with its inner void) who has no sense of belonging, self-esteem, or control must come to Him for fulfillment and satisfaction of all those deep needs of the human soul.

In verse 37 Jesus proceeds to address the problem of the rejected self: "All that the Father gives me will come to me, and whoever comes to me I will never drive away." Jesus promises that He will never reject those who come to Him. And then in verse 40 Jesus speaks of the re-creation of the whole person: "For my Father's will is that everyone who looks to the Son and believes in him shall have eternal life, and I will raise him up at the last day." We have here a comforting pledge of absolute security—the deficiencies of the needing self totally filled by the

Bread of Life, the rejected self now unconditionally accepted, the whole person re-created!

Romans 8 is another passage which deals with the problems inherent in both parts of the divided self. In verse 15 we read that we have "received the Spirit of sonship. And by him we cry, 'Abba, Father.' " The term *Abba*, which is not translated since it is Aramaic rather than Greek, was the small child's word for "father." It connotes intimacy and respect. Jesus used it in His prayer in Gethsemane (Mark 14:36). Paul uses the term in Romans 8 to point out that by our adoption as God's children we have an intimate, affirmative relationship with Him. God has become our true parent, our real Father; we belong to Him as eternal members of His family. As such we regain self-esteem through the love demonstrated at Calvary and a sense of control through the indwelling of the Holy Spirit. Thus in the *Abba*-relationship all of the deficiencies of the needing self find fulfillment.

Likewise, Romans 8 deals with the rejected self. Having touched on our miserable condition resulting from the fall, the negative powers of the rejected self ("What a wretched man I am! Who will rescue me from this body of death?"—Rom. 7:24), Paul rejoices that "there is now no condemnation for those who are in Christ Jesus, because through Christ Jesus the law of the Spirit of life set me free from the law of sin and death" (Rom. 8:1–2). Nor will there be any separation "from the love of God that is in Christ Jesus our Lord" (v. 39). Once we are united with God through the work of Jesus, we are no longer in danger of being cast out, banished, rejected. The extraordinary negative powers of the rejected self are canceled. The problems of the divided self are totally eliminated (see Figure 17).

To restore human identity, it is necessary for God to address both aspects of the divided self. We have seen that God's adoption of us as His children, the love of Christ, and the eternal life He offers fill all the deficiencies of the needing self. But how did God address the problems of the rejected self? The answer is that Christ Himself took on our feelings of rejection. Early in His ministry, for example, Jesus as the second Adam was cast out into the wilderness to face the temptations of Satan. Unlike Adam, Christ did not fall and His unified self was not divided. Most significant, however, is that on the cross Jesus took on Himself

FIGURE 17 The Healing of the Divided Self

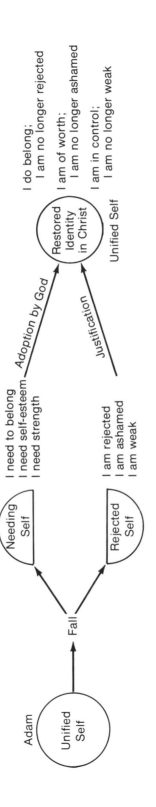

punishment, rejection, and shame. During those darkest hours between twelve and three Jesus suffered the very essence of the rejected self so that we would not have to endure it. Consequently, we can now be free from punishment, free from rejection, free from shame, free from all the results of the fall, all of which we deserve.

How do we appropriate this freedom from the negative powers of the rejected self? The apostle John tells us, "There is no fear in love. But perfect love drives out fear, because fear has to do with punishment. The man who fears is not made perfect in love" (1 John 4:18). The fear of punishment is, of course, an element of the rejected self. Christ's love cancels out our fear of punishment and abandonment. John is urging that we be perfected in Christ's love so that we might be free from the tyranny of anxiety. He is exhorting us to greater and greater intimacy in our relationship with Christ so that we might fully experience His love and that our needing self might thus find complete fulfillment. As we look to Jesus, the author and finisher of our faith, the rejected self with all its fears and anxieties will be abolished, and the needing self will move ever closer to Him.

Essentials in the Process of Restoring Identity

Finally, before closing our discussion of the basic process by which personal identity is restored, we note three components which must be present in our lives if that process is to reach completion: (1) compassion toward ourselves, (2) conviction, and (3) confession (see Figure 18).

FIGURE 18   Essentials in the Process of Restoring Identity

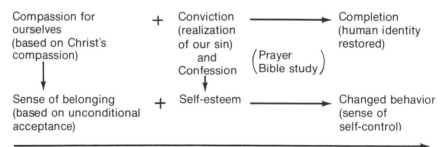

(1) We must have a compassion for ourselves which reflects Christ's compassion for us. Knowing that He unconditionally accepts us will help us to accept ourselves. This means accepting ourselves with both the good and bad which are within us. For Christ loves us as we are, and failure to love whom Christ loves is sin. Accepted by Christ and ourselves, we regain a sense of belonging.

(2) We must also have an awareness of, a conviction concerning, our sin. We must recognize those areas of our lives which are sinful and hinder our relationship with God. The important factor at this point is what we do with this knowledge. There is a danger that knowing what is bad about ourselves will undermine our acceptance of ourselves ("I am no good; therefore I must reject myself"). That must not be allowed to happen. The process of restoring human identity must not go into reverse. It is essential to remind ourselves that Christ, the perfect One, has accepted us and that our relationship with Him is forever sealed by His love.

(3) As we become aware of the problem areas in our lives, we must make confession of them to God. Prayer and Bible study are crucial here. We must commit the difficulty to God in prayer, asking Him to help us change and develop more-desirable behavior. In addition to assuring us of Christ's continuing love and acceptance, the Scriptures provide us with the motivation and the power to change. The Bible also gives us various patterns for change; that is, specific helps on how to correct particular areas of difficulty.

Self-acceptance, conviction concerning our sin, and confession to God will result in heightened self-esteem. And as we regain self-esteem, turn to God in prayer, and study His Word, our behavior will change. We will find ourselves in control. What Adam lost in the fall (a sense of belonging, self-esteem, and control) will have been restored. Human identity will once again be complete.

PART THREE

The Essentials of Christian Counseling

6

A Christian Model for Counseling
Imparting a Sense of Belonging

As a result of the restoration of human identity, the Christian can say: "I belong to God and can therefore trust; I am loved and can therefore experience self-esteem; I am in control and have hope." Our model for Christian counseling springs from this very sense of personal identity that God in His love has given us. In counseling others we can extend the love of God by helping them in turn to realize for themselves the firm sense of identity and inner security which we have.

Just as God the Father meets our needs for security and a sense of belonging, the family of believers centered around the Father is to relate to others so that they too might come to feel that "I belong and can therefore trust." Just as Christ meets our need for self-esteem, members of the body of Christ are to build up (edify) others and thereby bring them to the point where they can say, "I am loved and therefore experience self-esteem." Just as the Holy Spirit meets our need for strength, the church is to be characterized by service so that the weak or inadequate might gain a sense of power: "I am in control and have hope."

Figure 19 shows that there are three basic elements or stages in Christian counseling—imparting a sense of belonging ("you are part of God's family"), edification, and service. Note that they

FIGURE 19   The Three Stages in Christian Counseling

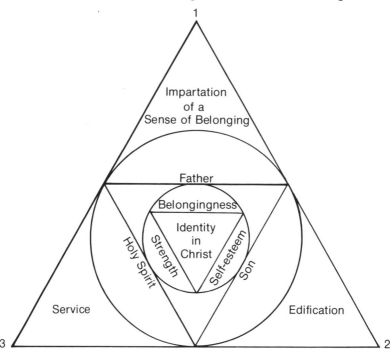

are not only related to the three basic needs which are fulfilled when human identity is restored, but they are also the major tasks of the church. We will find that the three elements of the counseling process build on each other: imparting a sense of belonging is foundational; edification and service follow.

Before we move into a detailed discussion of our model for counseling, however, it should be emphasized that our approach must resemble God's approach to Adam after the fall. God called to the man, "Where are you?" (Gen. 3:9). This is in contrast to the "there you are" approach so prevalent in much of evangelical Christianity. The truth, of course, is that we cannot know where other people are or what the real problems are unless we take the time to find out. Finding out where other people really are, which usually turns out to be far removed from the problem they initially presented, takes time, care, and commitment. Too many counselors think they have immediate biblical answers for everyone; they tend to say, "There you are," before they know what the real problem is. Job's counselors are excellent examples of the "there you are" approach—they ended up totally misrepresenting Job's position and God's attitude toward him. Surely no Christian wants to be guilty of giving false or wrong advice, or misapplying God's redemptive message. The best way to avoid such mistakes is, in effect, to ask, "Where are you? I want to understand what your problem really is." It is vital that on every level of interpersonal action the Christian community adopt a "where are you?" rather than a "there you are" approach.

Belonging to the Family of God

Imparting a sense of belonging is the most important aspect of effective counseling. Little constructive interaction can occur until the individual being counseled feels, "I belong to my counselor and my counselor belongs to me." The goal of this first stage of the process is to get the counselee to experience a sense of trust in the counselor and, eventually, a feeling of belonging to the family of God (see Figure 20).

At this point someone might legitimately ask what belongingness feels like. Milton Mayeroff gives an apt answer:

> What is "being with" like from the point of view of the one cared for when he realizes he is being cared for? When the other is with me, I feel I am not alone, I feel understood, not in some detached way, but because I feel he knows what it is like to be me. I realize that he wants to see me as I am, not in order to pass judgment on me, but to help me. I do not have to conceal myself by trying to appear better than I am; instead I can open up myself for him, let him get close to me. Realizing that he is with me helps me to see myself and my world more truly, just as someone repeating my words may give me the opportunity really to listen to myself and have the meaning of my own words come home to me more completely. [Mayeroff 1971, 43]

The Christian foundation for genuine belongingness is the doctrine of adoption. God the Father has personally adopted sons and daughters into His family, uniting individuals to Him and to each other in a mystical but dynamic way. Members of this family experience a new and special kind of belonging. It is significant

FIGURE 20   A Christian Model for Counseling—Stage 1

Stage 1

Imparting a Sense
of Belonging

(Where are you?)

Goal: To get counselees
to trust the counselor
and to feel that they are
part of God's family

1. Empathy
2. Genuineness
3. Warmth and Respect
4. Concreteness

Trust
and
Self-exploration

that the New Testament calls the church the household of God. The word *household*, which suggests some type of family structure, is one of the renderings of *oikos*. Six derivatives of *oikos* occur in Ephesians 2:19–22, a passage which sets forth the church as a community of Christian believers gathered or built around God.

> Consequently, you are no longer foreigners and aliens [*paroikol*], but fellow citizens with God's people and members of God's household [*oikeioi*], built on [*epoikodométhentes*] the foundation of the apostles and prophets, with Christ Jesus himself as the chief cornerstone. In him the whole building [*oikodomé*] is joined together and rises to become a holy temple in the Lord. And in him you too are being built together [*sunoikodomeisthe*] to become a dwelling [*katoikétérion*] in which God lives by his Spirit.

Paul here uses the metaphor of a building, a temple, to express the spiritual unity of Christians. The image of an eternal spiritual family in which we are full members is crucial to Christian doctrine and practice. Through Jesus there is a place for everyone in God's household.

Paul had introduced the subject of family earlier in Ephesians when he said, "[God] predestined us to be adopted as his sons through Jesus Christ, in accordance with his pleasure and will" (Eph. 1:5). In Ephesians 2, after noting that members of the church are no longer foreigners but citizens, he narrows his focus by designating them "members of God's household." Personal relationships within the family of God are much more intense than the general, external relationships offered by citizenship in a particular state. The latter are impersonal and legal; the family provides blood relationships. The term *household* suggests the degree of intimacy God desires with us.

But the love which distinguishes the family of God transcends even blood relationships. Jesus' words to the disciples at the Last Supper show His concern for the unity of God's family. He specifies love as the key element of our life together. Our standard for love is to be God's love:

> As the Father has loved me, so have I loved you. Now remain in my love. . . . My command is this: Love each other as I have loved you. Greater love has no one than this, that one lay down his life for his friends. . . . This is my command: Love each other. [John 15:9, 12–13, 17]

Paul offers another picture of the love within God's family: "We were gentle among you, like a mother caring for her little children. We loved you so much that we were delighted to share with you not only the gospel of God but our lives as well, because you had become so dear to us" (1 Thess. 2:7b–8).

Creation of a sense of family love or belongingness is not an option but a command. The command is totally compatible with a believer's new identity in Christ. We are to show forth such love as Christ Himself modeled in the midst of the disciples. We can impart a strong sense of "I belong to you" and "you belong to me" through the mystical union of God's family. We can trust each other completely because we are brothers and sisters in Jesus Christ, our "elder brother."

The deep human need for a sense of belonging is already clear in the story of Adam:

> But no matter how richly favored and how grateful, that first man was not satisfied, not fulfilled. The cause is indicated to him by God Himself. It lies in his solitude. It is not good for the man that he should be alone. He is not so constituted, he was not created that way. His nature inclines to the social—he wants company. He must be able to express himself, reveal himself, and give himself. He must be able to pour out his heart, to give form to his feelings. He must share his awareness with a being who can understand him and can feel and live along with him. Solitude is poverty, forsakenness, gradual pining and wasting away. How lonesome it is to be alone! [Bavinck 1956, 188]

Without a sense of belonging, Christians are prone to stagnate, develop emotional problems, and generally become ineffective. Drawing on personal experience, psychiatrist Herbert Wagemaker has poignantly expressed the need for belongingness within the Christian community:

> The Christian community lies undiscovered, dormant—and many basic needs go unmet. . . . This was a problem for me at one time in my Christian life. I struggled with anxieties, feelings of dissatisfaction and incompleteness, and I felt that few of my Christian friends really knew me. I was all alone in my walk with the Lord, or at least felt I was. I couldn't share my doubts about my faith or the teachings of the church; these were written off as spiritual problems and I was advised to deal with them on that level.
>
> My overwhelming need was for a sense that I was not alone in the Lord; I needed a forerunner to share my life—my whole life—with other Christians. I continued to struggle with these feelings until I stumbled onto the concept of Christian community. This is not unique to me—others had made the discovery long before I did. But although the concept has been with us since Jesus molded the disciples around such an interaction, churches and individuals by and large have failed to grasp so basic an idea. [Wagemaker 1978, 21–22]

Essential Factors in Creating a Sense of Belonging

Following biblical mandates, the Christian friend or counselor must impart a strong feeling of oneness with the counselee. An open relationship is necessary, with a commitment to care. It is essential that the counselor display (1) *empathy*, (2) *genuineness*, and (3) *warmth* if the counselee is to develop a sense of belonging. Indeed, studies have shown that effective counselors, regardless of their theoretical orientation, exhibit these qualities. Empathy, genuineness, and warmth are central ingredients of successful therapy.

> Several common threads weave their way through almost every major theory of psychotherapy and counseling. . . . All have emphasized the importance of the therapist's ability to be integrated, mature, genuine, authentic or congruent in his relationship to the patient. They have all stressed . . . the importance of the therapist's ability to provide a non-threatening, trusting, safe or secure atmosphere by his acceptance, non-possessive warmth, unconditional positive regard or love. Finally, virtually all theories of psychotherapy emphasize that for the therapist to be helpful he must be accurately empathetic, be "with" the client, be understanding, or grasp the patient's meaning. . . . These three sets of characteristics can, for lack of better words, be termed accurate empathy, non-possessive warmth, and genuineness. [Truax and Carkhuff 1967, 25]

1. Empathy

The helping process must be characterized first of all by empathy, putting oneself in the shoes of another, seeing the world as that person sees it without imposing one's own values or interpretations. If others are going to trust, they must feel that they are listened to and that they are understood. The counselor can induce that feeling in the client by placing himself or herself in the client's frame of reference.

As much as possible, counselors must suspend their own frame of reference. The counselee's logic, even if it is weak or foolish, must be understood by the listener. Empathy means "understanding from the internal frame of reference, rather than from the external or so-called objective frame of reference" (Hammond 1977, 3).

Empathetic understanding means sensitive perception of what another person is experiencing. Going beyond simple facts and circumstances, it is the ability to sense another's anxiety, fear, depression, numbness, confusion, tenderness, love, or care as if the emotion were one's own. To experience the identical emotion felt by the counselee is of course impossible. Rather, the helper is to be thought of as the "other self" or "alter ego" of the one being helped. The two walk arm in arm as it were, with the helper imparting care, understanding, and support of the other's emotional experience.

Only when empathetic understanding is shown can the confused and suffering person find the strength to explore those thoughts and feelings which cause shame or fear.

> As the patient moves tentatively toward feelings and experiences that he experiences as shameful, fearful, or even terrifying, the therapist steps into the patient's shoes and takes him one step further in self-exploration, doing so in a self-accepting and congruent manner that lessens the patient's own fears of coming to grips with the experiences or feelings. [Truax and Carkhuff 1967, 285]

In assisting a troubled person to identify and explore feelings, the counselor may also help the individual to sense attitudes of which he or she may be entirely unaware. This must be done in such a way as not to uncover feelings that would be too threatening.

Sometimes the counselor might hesitate to acknowledge strong conscious feelings of the one being helped for fear that verbalization of those emotions might intensify them. Yet the counselor must acknowledge them. It is important that the counselee understand that the counselor will not be threatened by the exploration of such feelings. The counselor should never avoid exploring what an individual expressly feels for fear the client cannot take it. The person is already taking it! The question is: Will the counselee be allowed to work it out with the counselor, or must the counselee endure it alone?

Existential (humanist) and psychoanalytic schools stress that empathy is "being with" the counselee, that is, understanding and being close to the client. The focus is on being with and staying with the feelings of the counselee. To actually feel and be emotionally aroused by what the client is feeling is termed "affective empathy." Carl Rogers and others define empathy as accurate perception of what the counselee is feeling and communication of that perception. That kind of empathy, which relates to a therapist's perceptual and communication skills, is called "cognitive empathy."

The two types of empathy, affective and cognitive, can be located on a continuum representing the interpersonal distance between counselor and counselee (see Figure 21). When displaying cognitive empathy, the counselor is still at a considerable distance from the client. In the case of affective empathy the therapist's own feelings have been stirred to resemble those of the client, so the interpersonal distance is reduced (Lewis 1978, 32–35). Good therapists manifest both types of empathetic skills during counseling sessions.

Counselors who fail in empathetic skills fall into five groups:

1. The marginal empathizer, who penetrates only a part of the patient's experience.
2. The evangelical therapist who is so concerned with changing the patient that he or she often fails to empathize effectively.
3. The hysteric empathizer, who overidentifies in a symbiotic way.
4. The compulsive empathizer, who can identify with one ego state of the patient but cannot easily shift to identify with another.
5. The rationalistic empathizer, who cannot abandon his or her professional role and underidentifies with the patient. [Lewis 1978, 41]

FIGURE 21   Cognitive and Affective Empathy

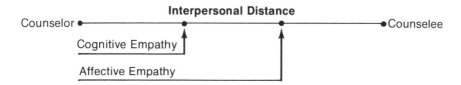

Regrettably, some Christian counselors discount the importance of empathy. Others seem unaware of its importance. Jay Adams states that he limits his discussion of empathy (as defined here) because "the Bible is overtly slim on the subject. I believe that this scriptural silence may be accounted for in one way only; the Bible does not emphasize empathy for exactly the same reason that I do not—*there is no need to do so*" (Adams 1977, 25). Adams's statement that the Bible says little concerning empathy ignores the New Testament synonyms for "empathize" which are used to describe God's working in His creation and among His people: (1) to be fully aware of, (2) to be attuned to, (3) to abandon oneself in, (4) to be caught up in, (5) to be immersed in, (6) to share or participate in, (7) to respond to, (8) to forget oneself in, (9) to be absorbed by, (10) to blend oneself with (Oden 1978, 54).

The incarnation is the greatest example of empathy. "The Word became flesh and lived for a while among us" (John 1:14). In becoming human, Christ gave up equality with God and humbled Himself even to the point of death. We might say that Christ left His own frame of reference—the very presence of the Godhead— and entered another frame of reference—the human world. Christ entered our fallen and sinful world. At no point did He distance Himself from the problems, miseries, and heartaches of those around Him. Far from being a spectator, He experienced the temptations and pressures of humankind yet remained without sin.

B. B. Warfield points out that "in the accounts which the evangelists give us of the crowded activities which filled the few years of [Jesus'] ministry, the play of a great variety of emotions is depicted." The emotion most often attributed to Jesus Christ is that of compassion, "an internal movement of pity" springing from the heart (Warfield 1950, 96ff.). "When he saw the crowds, he had compassion on them, because they were harassed and helpless, like sheep without a shepherd" (Matt. 9:36). "All Christ's healing work cost Him feeling" (Stalker 1891, 57). Jesus Himself referred to His love: "As the Father has loved me, so have I loved you. Now remain in my love" (John 15:9).

An excellent example of Jesus' empathy is to be found in John 11. Having heard that His close friend Lazarus was seriously ill, Jesus journeyed from across the Jordan to Bethany. Now Bethany was near Jerusalem, where there had very recently been an attempt to stone Him (John 10:31). Yet when He saw the sorrow of Mary, Martha, and the other mourners, there was no trace of preoccupation with either weariness from the journey or the danger to His life. Rather, Jesus wept. It is clear that His weeping was induced by empathetic identification with the mourners. "When Jesus saw [Mary] weeping, and the Jews who had come along with her also weeping, he was deeply moved in spirit and troubled. ... Jesus wept" (John 11:33, 35). Christ's empathetic response caused the Jews standing nearby to say, "See how he loved him [Lazarus]" (John 11:36).

Empathy permeated Christ's life. He understood the human plight because He became a human person Himself. He allowed Himself to experience our distresses, but He went beyond that. Through the punishment He bore on the cross He also experienced the totality of God's wrath, which rightfully belongs to us because of our sin. Christ endured the condemnation due us so that by trusting Him we would not have to experience it ourselves.

The incarnation and ministry of Christ prompted the author of Hebrews to write, "For we do not have a high priest who is unable to sympathize with our weaknesses, but we have one who has been tempted in every way, just as we are—yet was without sin" (Heb. 4:15). The word *sympathize* (literally, "to suffer alongside of"), like *empathy,* is very graphic. Christ's suffering was all-inclusive with regard to human weaknesses ("in every way"). The example of Christ's work of redeeming humanity is set before us as we attempt to understand and care for others.

2. Genuineness

The second essential factor in creating a sense of belonging is genuineness. This means that counselors are to "be themselves" as they relate to their clients.

> The therapist is "for real," an open, honest, sincere person. He is involved in the relationship and not simply a mirror, a sounding board or a blank screen. He is a real person in a real encounter. And that is the reason why the exact nature of the relationship cannot be predicted or controlled in advance. He is freely and deeply himself, without a façade, not phony. [Patterson 1974, 62]

To be genuine or congruent, counselors must accurately reflect what they are internally, as long as doing so does not hurt the counselee. It is virtually impossible for a feeling of closeness or belonging to develop if a helper is not genuine. Humans seem intuitively to recoil from people whom they perceive as playing a role. If an individual senses that another is not being completely open, anxiety develops; there is a disturbance in the exchange of signals which determine the nature of the relationship. In a professional situation a dominant-submissive pattern is almost automatic, an inherent barrier to openness and authentic relating. For that reason it is vital that counselors be genuine. Although they might prefer to be detached and distant, to control the situation, the Bible does not allow role playing.

Transparency seems to come only with great difficulty for many in the Christian community and especially for its leaders. Being a Christian implies holding certain beliefs. Sometimes the counselor's theological training or knowledge of biblical doctrine becomes an obstacle to transparency. Those being counseled may be viewed simply as sponges that need to absorb truth; there is little consideration for their humanity and personhood. In a sincere desire to see others embrace Christian truths, a helper may become, as it were, an impersonal computer with a Bible verse or doctrinal answer for every problem. In such sessions the troubled person senses little genuineness or care.

Throughout the twentieth century, evangelical Christianity has been preoccupied with contending for propositional truth as revealed in Scripture. The price paid for militantly maintaining biblical truth has cost the church dearly in other areas, especially the interpersonal. "As a result the conservative Christian community [has been] more oriented around content than companionship, doctrine than fellowship, intake than interaction, study than sharing" (Howard 1979, 165). Impersonal application of meticulously studied doctrine may actually be an attempt to hide from congruence and reality. It may be a cover-up for fear of stripping away professional image. Clearly, one hiding person is of little help to another hiding person. Cold doctrinal transmission may also signify lack of personal concern. But the imparting of Christian truth must be a help to healing, not a hindrance. Successful Christian counselors do not merely know and recite doctrine—like Jesus and Paul they live it!

Christian helpers must make a commitment to being genuine and transparent persons, leaving behind roles, masks, and defensiveness. In their search to see other people as they really are, counselors must be willing to be seen as they themselves are. Then the fullness of the Christian message can be applied within a personal, warm, and healing relationship. Such a relationship provides the client a unique opportunity for growth and personal exploration. A transparent helper can be the catalyst for the client to open up. For that reason the helper should give clear and honest feedback to counselees. Such feedback makes them aware of their impact on at least one other person. We must not be afraid to communicate genuine responses to those we seek to help.

In being genuine, counselors show a personal strength that can risk hurt. Their example encourages those clients who are afraid to expose their actual selves lest they be discovered (both by themselves and by others). They may dare to face the truth only in the presence of a strong and caring person who has led the way in having the courage to be vulnerable.

> The client who senses the inner congruence of the therapist, who knows he is in the presence of one who is in touch with himself and experiences himself fully as he encounters estrangement, may be powerfully awakened to the possibility of congruence with himself. Meeting a living embodiment of self-reconciliation (albeit of a limited, imperfect order), the client nevertheless becomes newly aware of the promise of reconciliation with himself, openness to himself, which may have seemed an impossibility before therapy. The very process of dwelling for a time in the presence of a congruent person is itself undoubtedly a healing force. [Oden 1978, 57]

Jesus Christ's forthrightness and honesty contrasted with the behavior of the Pharisees, whom He called hypocrites (i.e., stage players). Sensing His genuineness, the common people heard Him gladly. "When Jesus had finished saying these things [the Sermon on the Mount], the crowds were amazed at his teaching, because he taught as one who had authority, and not as their teachers of the law" (Matt. 7:28–29).

One is also struck by the flexibility Jesus demonstrated in His ministry. He served variously as prophet, pastor, or priest according to the situation and the individuals with whom He was dealing. Currently, much of the evangelical church seems to view counseling as only a prophetic or confrontational ministry. Jay Adams (1970, 41–77) chastises ministers for preaching one way and counseling another, contending that only the prophetic role is appropriate for biblical counselors. It would be better for the Christian church to be guided by the model of counseling Jesus presented.

The writer to the Hebrews impresses on us the genuineness of Christ:

> In the past God spoke to our forefathers through the prophets at many times and in various ways, but in these last days he has spoken to us by his Son, whom he appointed heir of all things, and through whom he made the universe. The Son is the radiance of God's glory and the exact representation of his being, sustaining all things by his powerful word. [Heb. 1:1–3]

Note especially the description of Jesus Christ as the exact representation of God's being.

The apostle Paul was also genuine. He observed that the mature Christian always speaks the truth in love (Eph. 4:15). Pouring out his own hurt to Timothy, Paul wrote, "At my first defense, no one came to my support, but everyone deserted me. May it not be held against them" (2 Tim. 4:16). He cried for companionship: "Do your best to come to me quickly. . . . Do your best to get here before winter" (2 Tim. 4:9, 21). At other times he could scathingly confront people: "I am astonished that you are so quickly deserting the one who called you by the grace of Christ. . . . You foolish Galatians! Who has bewitched you?" (Gal. 1:6; 3:1). Yet in rebuking those who had gone astray, he never belittled them. Whatever the situation, what Paul showed to others was his true self.

Of course, the necessity of being genuine with others does not mean that a counselor may adopt an "anything goes" policy. That a counselor must show his or her true self does not give license to express anger or hostility indiscriminately. It does not entitle Christians to attack, under the guise of righteous indignation, people who do not respond as they want them to.

> Many persons are . . . destructive when they are genuine. Again genuineness is not to be confused, as is so often done, with free license for the therapist to do what he will in therapy, especially to express hostility. Therapy is not for the therapist. [Patterson 1974, 63]

This note of caution needs to be heard and acted upon. Many Christians have been devastated by hostile remarks which other believers make in the name of truth or love. Some very dedicated Christians, for example, because they take psychology seriously and try to integrate it with Scripture, have been labeled "sugar-coated Skinnerians" or "profoundly ignorant of the Scriptures." And many other Christians have, in the name of truth or principle, been the target of torrents of anger because of some minor doctrinal difference. Those who unfairly attack others in this way feel their admonitions are justified. In most cases they have little awareness that what they are doing is only a caricature of "speaking the truth in love." They need to be reminded of Paul's eloquent definition of love:

> Love is patient, love is kind. It does not envy, it does not boast, it is not proud. It is not rude, it is not self-seeking, it is not easily angered, it keeps no record of wrongs. Love does not delight in evil but rejoices with the truth. It always protects, always trusts, always hopes, always perseveres. Love never fails. [1 Cor. 13:4–8]

This definition lays a foundation for genuineness. Only a person who embodies ideal love will find it possible and fitting to be completely transparent in relationships with others.

3. Warmth

A difficult characteristic for Christian helpers to develop is warmth or respect. This is the ability to esteem others while at the same time refusing to accept their unsatisfactory thoughts, feelings, and behavior. The tendency in evangelical Christianity has been to reject those who do not conform to biblical standards (and, just as often, extrabiblical standards) rather than to show them care and concern.

Respect involves unconditional positive regard for the one being helped. For therapeutic change to occur, the person in need must feel prized by the helper.

> Caring, prizing, valuing and liking are other terms for the respect condition. It is a non-possessive caring. The client is regarded as a person of worth; he is respected. The counselor's attitude is non-

evaluative, non-judgmental, without criticism, ridicule, deprecia-
tion or reservations. This does not mean that the counselor accepts
as right, desirable or likable all aspects of the client's behavior or
that he agrees with or condones all his behavior. In the non-
judgment attitude the [therapist] does not relinquish his own sense
of values, his personal or social ethics. Yet the client is accepted
for what he is, as he is. There is no demand or requirement that
he change or be different in order to be accepted or that he be
perfect. Imperfections are accepted, along with mistakes and errors, as part of the human condition. [Patterson 1974, 58]

A nonjudgmental attitude on the part of the helper does not imply
condoning unsatisfactory behavior. One is not to be false or un-
genuine to those whose actions are displeasing or substandard.
The helper, however, must see beyond negative attitudes or behaviors to what lies below them. This will entail asking questions like "Why is this person so destructive and hostile?" or
"What is it that makes this person so quiet and withdrawn?"

The individual being counseled must be seen as a unified whole
rather than as a collection of behaviors some of which the therapist may not like. Respect for the client focuses on the inner
person or the heart. Understanding the internal dynamics underlying symptoms like insecurity or defensiveness helps a therapist
to see the basic worth of the one being counseled. The counselor
should visualize clients in the context of all the environmental
factors that created their present makeup, including family,
friends, church, and school. With such a perspective, one can
view counselees as they really are and then accept and love them
in their present emotional condition. It is important to see beyond the immediate behavior.

The counselor should always keep the principle of reciprocal
affect in view—we all respond to warmth with warmth and to
hostility with hostility. This principle, basic to all of life, is evident already in the behavior of a baby. Helpless and dependent,
a baby, just like adolescents and adults, responds in kind to love
and tenderness as well as to rejection and hostility.

In putting forth this principle, psychologists are echoing biblical truths. Respect and warmth are basic to the Christian message. God's grace is free—we do not merit it through good deeds.
God's grace cannot be earned; rather, He shows undeserved love
to His children. His grace was shown primarily in the atoning

death of Christ, God's demonstration of unconditional love for people who were alienated from Him. In dying on the cross Christ was saying in effect, "I love you as you are—rebellious, hating, sinful—and I am willing to bear hell's wrath for you." While He does not condone sin, He nonetheless loves us sinners. He does not demand that we reform ourselves, but instead works our transformation Himself.

Scripture notes that we respond to God because of what God has done for us. This is a perfect example of the principle of reciprocal affect. The apostle John says, "We love because he first loved us" (1 John 4:19). Paul underscores the same theme. "For Christ's love compels us, because we are convinced that one died for all, and therefore all died. And he died for all, that those who live should no longer live for themselves but for him who died for them and was raised again" (2 Cor. 5:14–15). Those verses capture the essence of Scripture. God has approached the human person with *agapē* love and grace. We are to respond in kind.

One of the outworkings of this central Christian doctrine will be a corresponding respect and warmth in the counseling process. "Even as God unconditionally loves the sinner in order to free him from self-righteousness, anxiety, guilt and defensiveness ... so in effective therapy does the client experience in some sense what appears to be a relationship of unconditional positive regard" (Oden 1978, 74). The Christian counselor must remember that the client's outward behavior does not always clearly reflect the inner self. Accordingly, the therapist must not judge an individual's essence in terms of performance nor worth in terms of works. Christ's atonement shows that God did not value us according to our performance—if He had, we would have been hopelessly lost. Rather, the cross declares that despite our works we are loved unconditionally just as we are.

In showing respect for others, the Christian counselor mirrors Christ's attitude. To illustrate the principle "in humility consider others better than yourselves" (Phil. 2:3), Paul broke into a hymn describing Christ's humiliation and exaltation (vv. 6–11). To the Romans Paul wrote, "Love must be sincere. ... Be devoted to one another in brotherly love. Honor one another above yourselves" (Rom. 12:9–10). To the Galatians he said, "If someone is caught in a sin, you who are spiritual should restore him gently. But watch yourself, or you also may be tempted" (Gal. 6:1). And once again we should mention his definition of love in 1 Corinthians 13. If the counselor shows love, warmth, and respect, the client will reciprocate.

Unfortunately, evangelical counseling today is in large measure not characterized by an unconditional acceptance of counselees. Rather, the nouthetic school emphasizes confrontation, which carries a high risk of rejecting the one being counseled. Counselees have the fear that inability to change or give up a "sinful habit pattern" will prompt rejection. And, indeed, if the client does not follow the directive of the counselor—which is the heart of the nouthetic system—what else can the counselor do?

The whole nouthetic method, with its emphasis on being prophetic or exhortational, makes it difficult for the counselor to show respect for the one being helped. "The nouthetic counselor cannot listen or accept clients' sinful attitudes or verbalizations since the 'acceptance of sin is sin.' . . . Consequently, support as conceived of by psychology or psychiatry is unacceptable" (Carter 1975, 150).

Some nouthetic teachings are difficult to reconcile with Paul's call to restore the sinner gently (Gal. 6:1). At the very least, the nouthetic emphasis places the counselor in a dominant position requiring the counselee to be submissive. A dominant-submissive structure within the counseling relationship will prevent establishment of a sense of truly belonging to each other. Furthermore, the one being counseled may be motivated to change in order to please the counselor rather than to please God.

Evangelical thought has moved in a healthy direction in recognizing the worth of the human person. Individuals have value by virtue of creation. By contrast, humanism has no basis for assigning worth to a person because under that system God has been displaced as the measure of all things. Evangelical thought goes far beyond humanism by declaring that individuals have worth because they are created in the image of God. Although fallen, we still possess a remnant of that image which gives us true value. No person is a zero, a nothing.

On the other hand, there has also been some unhealthy movement amid evangelical thought. Emphases such as those of Jay Adams, for example, have a tendency to overlook the universality of the fall. Human sinfulness applies to both counselee and counselor. An attitude that precludes a listening ear or support as the counselee tries to come to grips with sinful behavior unduly elevates the counselor and lowers the counselee. The result is a lack of togetherness and of the respect necessary for a sense of belonging to occur.

4. Concreteness

In addition to the three qualities (empathy, genuineness, warmth) which are generally recognized as indispensable ingredients of a counseling relationship that successfully imparts a sense of belonging, we must also mention concreteness. Concreteness is getting to the specifics. It is the use of specific rather than general or abstract terminology to describe feelings, experiences, and behavior. By avoiding vagueness and ambiguity, we pinpoint feelings and experiences rather than generalizing them. A counselor can help a person with self-exploration by encouraging identification of specific troublesome feelings, experiences, or behavior. It is important for the counselor to be concrete in responding even when the counselee is vague.

A counselor who responds in a vague way or who does not require the counselee to be specific may allow vast areas of feelings or experience to pass by without an inquiry that would force the counselee to recognize their full significance. This dimension of counseling may appear to be self-evident, but sessions conducted by a beginning counselor are often ineffective because they lack concreteness. There are basically three functions which concreteness accomplishes in the counseling process:

1. It keeps the therapist's response close to the client's feelings and experiences.
2. It fosters accurate understanding by the therapist, allowing for early client corrections of misunderstanding.
3. It encourages the client to attend to specific problem areas. [Patterson 1974, 68]

The therapist is to stay with exactly what the counselee is saying and feeling, which calls for focused listening. Without focused listening, the basic skill in creating a sense of belonging, a counselor cannot know where an individual is emotionally, cognitively, or spiritually. After asking "Where are you?" the helper must concentrate on the responses of the counselee, which may be veiled out of fear to reveal one's real self. Being a good listener is often difficult for people trained in theology or Bible doctrine. The feeling that one has all the answers or knows just what the counselee needs tends to produce hurried responses. That in turn closes the door to further exploration and understanding.

Much of what a therapist might ordinarily put into a counseling session works against active listening: ordering and directing, warning and threatening, moralizing and preaching, teaching and lecturing, advising and offering solutions, criticizing and judging, praising and flattering, name-calling, reassuring, psychoanalyzing, probing and questioning, using sarcasm and humor (Gordon 1975, 10–13). Sometimes such methods may be helpful or even necessary. But in general they do not help a counselor to listen with focused attention to the client.

We might also mention here a number of particular responses to avoid:

1. The soothing generalization: "You are not alone in this; there are few people in such a situation as this who would dare to say they have enough faith. Think for a moment of Christ in Gethsemane."
2. The well-meaning belittling: "But in the circumstances there's nothing wrong in recognizing a moment of doubt."
3. The fatherly moralization: "I can think of worse things than a moment's doubt before an operation."
4. Dogmatizing: "You mustn't forget that in Gethsemane Christ also asked that the cup be taken from Him."
5. Reacting to the content of the spoken words and avoiding the feelings: "Yes, you are depressed, but don't give in to feelings. Get up and get something done during the mornings."
6. Diagnosing, interpreting: "Because you feel a struggle in yourself, you're feeling guilty and afraid you'll give in to sin." [Faber and van der Schoot 1962, 74]

In other words, once the question "Where are you?" has been asked, the only proper tactic for the counselor is active and focused listening for the answer.

What are the hallmarks of the good listener? One of the requisites is that the helper be open and vulnerable, for only then can there be true empathy with another. A good listener fights down the impulsive response and takes time to understand the other person, to see the full implication of what is being said. The wise counselor will take time to question and get the client to clarify the details of events and experiences in order that concrete therapeutic communication geared specifically to the individual situation can be established. Being a good listener requires discipline. Counselors who really want to listen must for the time being forget their own personal affairs. Undivided attention must be given to listening.

The good listener insists on concreteness of language. This safeguards against the distorted perceptions which can result from the use of abstract, subjective terms. Even though there may be an earnest desire to understand the other person, concreteness is necessary because there are so many variables in human communication. Those variables influence the sending and receiving of messages and the encoding and decoding process. Concreteness reduces the risk of misunderstanding.

In this day of television, superficiality, and compulsive activity, we tend not to concentrate. But good listening requires concentration! During conversation, the counselor must pay rapt attention to the counselee. Through eye contact, an alert posture, and verbal acknowledgments of what has been said the counselor indicates to counselees that they are being carefully attended to.

Good listening demands active participation, a mind-set of relaxed alertness. Thomas Gordon uses the phrase "active listening." The counselor is not a passive listening post but is active in the process. The good listener interjects in order to clarify the ambiguous and acknowledge the flow of conversation. By being an active listener, the counselor is showing empathy and is assuring the client, "I am with you; I hear what you are saying, and I can feel with you." The active listener does not get lost trying to remember every fact, but focuses on the significance of what is being said. This assures that the counselee is not only being heard but understood as well. Being understood is essential for the amount of trust required if the counselee is to develop a sense of belonging.

Good listening helps to keep the counselor's responses close to the counselee's feelings and experiences, permitting correction of any misunderstanding the counselor may have. The active listener is open to being corrected. When answering the counselor's question, "Where are you?" the counselee must have the freedom to correct any misapprehensions by saying, "No, not there; I am over here." Often such freedom is not allowed in Christian counseling. The counselee's problems are forced into preconceived molds or categories. The theological points made by the counselor may be accurate, precise, and even profound, but they still may not fit the counselee's problems. If the counselor is to know the right doctrine to apply (as Jesus always did), it is essential to understand exactly where the counselee is.

Self-Exploration

The goal of imparting a sense of belonging is to give the counselee a sufficient amount of security to allow for self-exploration. It is frequently impossible to face one's innermost thoughts, the truth about oneself, alone. With the care and support of another, however, it is possible to venture into the dark places of the heart and face whatever exists there.

> Self-exploration reveals inconsistencies and contradictions. Attitudes and feelings that have been experienced but denied to awareness are discovered. Experiences inconsistent with the self-concept, or self-image, previously denied or distorted, become symbolized in awareness. The client becomes more open to his experiences. [Patterson 1974, 128]

Self-exploration is often best carried on in the presence of others who can be objective and bring new insights.

The ultimate source for insight about ourselves is, of course, God's revelation. His Word is "living and active. Sharper than any double-edged sword, it penetrates even to dividing soul and spirit" (Heb. 4:12). Yet, unfortunately, many members of the evangelical church, which has long emphasized those words, have done little self-exploring and changing. Verbal testimonies to the power of God's Word are sometimes spoken by persons who demonstrate an unchanging spirit of anger and hostility, criticism and gossip, or rigidity and phariseeism year after year. They show little or no personal growth. They certainly do not explore themselves to the extent that David asked God to examine him: "Search me, O God, and know my heart; test me and know my anxious thoughts" (Ps. 139:23). They may be open to self-exploration, but only in the presence of caring healers who reflect God's willingness to be drawn into human suffering.

It is well to reiterate at this point that, following God's example, we are to ask those who need help, "Where are you?" We must ask because in our fallibility we do not know where others are and can gain understanding only by listening. Hurting individuals can begin to gain some sense of exactly where they are only as they interact with another who cares. Without a commitment by some caring person there is usually little hope that hurting individuals will look within and stop their flight from reality and from God. They will continue to rely on their internal defense mechanisms, which are largely unconscious. To be able to function smoothly, they will choose to remain at a level where they can continue to hide from themselves. Under such circumstances the chances are very slim that they will be willing to take an inward journey on their own.

Regrettably, many counselors in evangelical circles today begin with the "there you are" approach. Such counselors do not see the importance of getting alongside another to gain an accurate understanding of the specific problems being presented. They feel that they already have the answers to whatever problems the individual may have. There is no basis for such an approach in the Bible. Indeed, the Book of Job stresses its perils.

Job—A Case Study

Job's faithfulness to God was severely tested. He lost his children, his possessions, and then his health. He was suffering inwardly, grieving over the loss of his children, as well as outwardly from the sores which afflicted his entire body. In this condition Job was approached by his three friends, Eliphaz, Bildad, and Zophar, who came to comfort him in his suffering. Upon seeing their friend Job, whom they hardly recognized, they wept and sat with him in silence for seven days.

Mistaking the silence of his friends for true empathy ("Where are you?"), Job expressed to them his real feelings, which can be summed up as a deep depression and a desire to die. "Why did I not perish at birth, and die as I came from the womb? . . . For sighing comes to me instead of food; my groans pour out like water. What I feared has come upon me; what I dreaded has happened to me. I have no peace, no quietness; I have no rest, but only turmoil" (Job 3:11, 24–26).

> [Job] is sick with despair—that sickness unto death of which Kierkegaard says the sufferer wishes to die but cannot. Why, he laments, should life be given to the bitter in soul? Why can it not all cease with death and at least the misery come to an end? He cannot follow his wife's cynical directive [to curse God and die] because he cannot honestly curse God. His religious problem is not that simple. At the same time he cannot honestly defend God. His trauma seems too unfair. So he is caught in the middle and in anguish asks why. [Hulme 1968, 26]

Job's plight simply cannot be explained and solved by human logic.

> Reason is our guide among the facts of life, but it does not give us the explanation of them. Sin, suffering, and the Book of God all bring a man to the realization that there is something wrong at the basis of life, and it cannot be put right by reason. Our Lord always dealt with the basement of life, i.e., with the real problem; if we only deal with the upper storey we do not realize the need of the Redemption, but once we hit the elemental line, everything becomes different. [Chambers 1931, 17]

Upon hearing Job express his feelings—an honest expression of where he really is—Eliphaz replies in such a condemnatory and nonempathetic manner that a deep cleavage between Job and his friends results. Apparently Eliphaz is incapable of helping Job. We gain some understanding of Eliphaz from his response to Job's exclamation of depression: "If someone ventures a word with you, will you be impatient? . . . But now trouble comes to you, and you are discouraged; it strikes you, and you are dismayed.

... Consider now: Who, being innocent, has ever perished? Where were the upright ever destroyed? ... at the blast of [God's] anger [the evil] perish. ... But if it were I, I would appeal to God; I would lay my cause before him" (Job 4:2, 5, 7, 9; 5:8).

> Threatened by Job's blast, [Eliphaz] attempted—perhaps compulsively—to silence him. He took the approach of the moralist who tries to motivate people by making them feel guilty. Even his offer to respect Job's freedom is quickly retracted. "If one ventures a word with you, will you be offended? Yet who can keep from speaking?" His speaking could be summed up by saying, "Shame on you, Job! Why can't you practice what you've preached?" [Hulme 1968, 28]

One important note here is Eliphaz's use of doctrinal or theological points. (This begins a long series of theological discourses by all three of the friends.) Eliphaz admonishes Job: "Blessed is the man whom God corrects; so do not despise the discipline of the Almighty. For he wounds, but he also binds up; he injures, but his hands also heal" (Job 5:17–18). This is certainly a superb point, a teaching which runs through all of revelation (see, e.g., Heb. 12:5–6). However, in this case it is spiritual counseling which misses the mark, for Job is not being corrected or disciplined by God. The words of advice have no positive effect on him because they do not speak to him where he is.

Eliphaz has basically brought forth a theological cause-and-effect formula: "You are suffering because you have sinned." But in Job's case the point is not valid and therefore causes him even greater humiliation and suffering. It is essential, then, for Christian helpers to be very slow to speak God's word amid situations which they do not as yet fully comprehend. When depression or anxiety strikes, the helper's primary function is to be supportive and listen. How often Christians suffering from depression have been perfunctorily told to keep their eyes on the Lord, confess their sin, renew their faith, be obedient to God, stop giving in to feelings! On and on the list goes. All of this is perfectly sound advice; but one must be absolutely sure, when giving such counsel, that it has direct application to the specific situation at hand. Eliphaz's counsel did not.

The reader knows, and Job believes, that what has happened is not punishment for some past sin. If there is a grain of truth in Eliphaz's teaching about the chastening of the Almighty (5:17), it is not in the negative sense of training so that a person is restrained from potential sin. Job had long since attained perfection in this stage of character development (1:1, 8; 2:3). The reader knows what Job does not know, namely, that Job's highest wisdom is to love God for Himself alone. Hence Eliphaz's words, far from being a comfort, are a trap. The violence with which Job rejects them shows his recognition of the danger. [Andersen 1976, 125]

After Eliphaz speaks, Job responds; and his response is very enlightening. He says that a person in despair should have the devotion of his friends, but he does not (Job 6:14–15). Job criticizes Eliphaz's poor performance. First Job notes that anxiety and fear have kept Eliphaz from being understanding and empathetic: "Now you too have proved to be of no help; you see something dreadful and are afraid" (Job 6:21).

Job is disappointed because the response of his friends has been insipid (vv. 5–7) and dry (vv. 15–20). . . . Job is rightly charging them with cowardice. Their cautious and conventional response betrays an unwillingness to get involved with a former friend who, they suspect, is now under the displeasure of God. There is a profound pastoral insight here; it is often fear that prevents a would-be counselor from attaining much empathy with his client. [Andersen 1976, 132]

Anxiety is a major hindrance to empathy because it turns the counselor inward rather than toward the one who needs help. The counselor becomes more concerned about his or her own needs (self-esteem, security) than the client's. Job's suffering has caused Eliphaz to wonder, "Will this happen to me, too? If it has happened to Job, why not to me?" (To interject a personal note: during counseling sessions I have occasionally found myself asking questions which detract from my ability to empathize. For example, a client may mention that a friend has cancer. My immediate response is to ask the age of the friend, hoping, of course, that I am many years younger. My own anxieties have been roused by the situation.)

Job continues his criticism: "How painful are honest words!

But what do your arguments prove? Do you mean to correct what I say, and treat the words of a despairing man as wind?" (Job 6:25–26). Job is striking an important note here. He is telling Eliphaz that logical arguments are of no help. Dealing with Job's misery strictly on a rational basis is to treat his words "as wind." Job is crying out to his friends, "I have emotions and feelings about everything that has happened to me. I'm depressed; I'm grieving, totally confused, and bewildered. But you want to cure me with logic. That shows you have completely misunderstood me."

> Job complains that his friends have dealt deceitfully as a brook [see Job 6:15–20], i.e., they have answered his words and not his meaning. . . . Job's anger seems to be of the order the apostle Paul mentions—"Be you angry and sin not" (Eph. 4:26). His anger was against the misunderstanding of his friends. He had a right to expect that they would not misunderstand. The reason they misunderstood was that they took Job's words and deliberately denied the meaning which they knew must be behind them, and that is a misunderstanding not to be easily excused. It is possible to convey a wrong impression by repeating the exact words of someone else, to convey a lie by speaking the truth, and this is the kind of misunderstanding Job indicates his friends are guilty of. They had stuck stedfastly to his literal words and taken their standpoint not from God, but from the creed they had accepted; consequently they not only criticize Job and call him bad, but they totally misrepresent God. Job's complaint is not the shallow expression often heard—"No one understands me." He is complaining of misunderstanding based on a misconstruction. He says in effect, You have given me counsel when I did not ask for it; I am too greatly baffled and can only hold to what I am persuaded of, viz., that I have not done wrong; but I am indignant with you for not understanding. [Chambers 1931, 27]

Job was not in need of rational theological discourse, but of someone who would understand and empathize with his emotional desperation. In responding to Eliphaz Job put his finger on the heart of many problems in the church: the relegation of feelings to a subordinate position and the mistaken notion that many normal human emotions are wrong and sinful. Today, Job would probably be given some trite advice—perhaps "You should be ruled by faith and not by your feelings," or "Take a good look at the facts and more appropriate feelings will follow." We have already pointed out in chapter 2, however, that the Bible regards the emotions of the heart as of paramount importance. This is particularly evident in the Book of Job.

Job and his friends totally missed each other because the friends did not empathize with him; they did not listen to where he was. He was operating primarily on the level of feelings, they on the level of facts and faith. He realized why they were talking past each other and tried to point it out, but the friends either could not or did not want to understand.

When a counselor makes a commitment to help another person, that commitment includes attempting to comprehend the other's emotions. It may well be that the person in need is overreacting and unhealthily dominated by feelings, but it will not help for the counselor to remain aloof and completely avoid those feelings. Just as Christ is willing to be involved in our emotions (He even endured our hostility and hatred toward Him to the point of being crucified and suffering the anguish of hell) in order to set them right, we too must become enmeshed in the emotional lives of others. Job's counselors were not willing to share Job's emotional misery. They became defensive and retreated. Consequently, they were utterly unable to help him.

Later on Job gives a devastating evaluation of all the counseling he has received: "What you know, I also know; I am not inferior to you. But I desire to speak to the Almighty and to argue my case with God. You, however, smear me with lies; you are worthless physicians, all of you! If only you would be altogether silent! For you, that would be wisdom" (Job 13:2–5). From Job's declaration that he knows the same theological arguments which his friends know and that he is not inferior to them we draw the conclusion that apparently they have been condescending, talking down to him with a holier-than-thou attitude. They are representative of the sort of

fanaticism which builds on one point of view only and is determinedly ignorant of everything else. . . . It is possible to build logical edifices on a theological position and at the same time to prove in practical life that the position is wrong. For example, on the metaphysical line the predestinations of God may seem clear,

but our conceptions of those predestinations may prove danger-
ously false when we come to the actual facts of life.

The theological view ought to be constantly examined; if we
put it in the place of God we become invincibly ignorant, that is,
we won't accept any other point of view, and the invincible ignorance of fanaticism leads to delusions for which we alone are to
blame. The fundamental things are not the things which can be
proved logically in practical life.

Watch where you are inclined to be invincibly ignorant, and you
will find your point of view causes you to break down in the most
vital thing. An accepted view of God has caused many a man to
fail at the critical moment; it has kept him from being the kind
of man he ought to be. Only when he abandons his view of God
for God Himself does he become the right kind of man. [Chambers
1931, 50]

It needs to be noted that neither Job nor the author of the
preceding quotation is attacking theology, but rather particular
mind-sets that value theology more highly than the presence of
God. Theological formulations, which are based to some extent
on human thinking, may be absolutely correct. Their correctness,
however, does not at all insure that they will lead to a deeper and
more intimate knowledge of God. Neither does their correctness
insure that they will be properly applied to human experience.
Job's counselors did not ask him, "Where are you?" As a result,
they ended up with a sinful misapplication of their theological
creed. Their condescending, inflexible mind-set kept them from
a true knowledge of both God and Job.

Job is thoroughly disgusted with his counselors. And justifiably
so. He is facing trials which are beyond their conception. This is
often the case when counselors take a "there you are" approach
and rush in with pat answers to problems and conflicts. In rebuking his friends, Job is in effect pleading, "Why don't you either
plunge into the depths with me, or else keep silent if you cannot
tell me what to do?" He accuses them of lying in their attempts
to defend God. This is a serious accusation. "Will you speak
wickedly on God's behalf? . . . Would it turn out well if he examined you?" (Job 13:7, 9). Concluding that all of them are worthless physicians, he turns to argue his case with God. Job's
statement in verse 15, "Though [God] slay me, yet will I hope in

him," shows that there is a depth in his relationship with God which his counselors obviously lack.

With the entrance of Elihu upon the scene (Job 32) the entire picture changes. Though his arguments to Job are not always theologically precise, he does show an entirely different spirit. He cares. His words reveal an empathy, an identification with Job's suffering. He is genuine in his approach; he does not play a role or condescend as so often happens in an office setting. He acknowledges that he is on the same level with Job: "I am just like you before God; I too have been taken from clay" (Job 33:6). Although Elihu is upset with Job for justifying himself rather than God, the young man's attitude nonetheless is one of warmth and respect. By setting an atmosphere in which Job can feel accepted, Elihu gives Job a sense of belonging and prepares him for his encounter with God.

The modern-day counselor would do well to follow the general example of Elihu. By creating an atmosphere which encourages trust the counselor can lead the client to a sense of belonging and the security necessary for self-exploration. Together they can then discuss the client's basic thoughts, feelings, and behavior as well as underlying causes and results.

7

A Christian Model for Counseling
Edification and Service

Edification

The second stage in our Christian model for counseling is edification, that is, strengthening the counselee's heart (the root meaning of the word is "building up"). "Each of us should please his neighbor for his good, to build him up" (Rom. 15:2). "Therefore encourage one another and build each other up, just as in fact you are doing" (1 Thess. 5:11).

The goal of edification is to help counselees gain a comprehensive self-understanding—an objective, healthy, and integrated perspective on their problems and on their assumptions about themselves, other people, and the world. In the process they will come to see that there is a need for them to make changes in their lives. As clients begin to view themselves more objectively, the counselor can help them to identify and actively apply to their lives hitherto unused (or underused) resources, especially biblical doctrines. The result will be significant positive change. As counselees internalize relevant Christian concepts, they will more fully realize the fact of their restored identity in Christ and thus be able to function more effectively (see Figure 22).

149

FIGURE 22   A Christian Model for Counseling—Stages 1 and 2

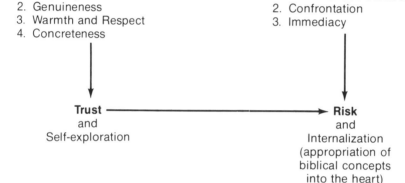

Stage 1

| Imparting a Sense of Belonging |

(Where are you?)

Goal: To get counselees
to trust the counselor
and to feel that they are
part of God's family

1. Empathy
2. Genuineness
3. Warmth and Respect
4. Concreteness

Trust
and
Self-exploration

Stage 2

| Edification |

(I love you)

Goal: To build up counselees
so they acquire insight into
and work through problems

1. Doctrinal Self-Disclosure
2. Confrontation
3. Immediacy

Risk
and
Internalization
(appropriation of
biblical concepts
into the heart)

Essential Components of Christian Edification

1. Doctrinal Self-Disclosure

There are three essential components of Christian edification: (1) doctrinal self-disclosure, (2) confrontation, and (3) immediacy. Secular therapists label the first component simply "self-disclosure." In self-disclosure therapists reveal appropriate information about themselves, including some of their ideas, feelings, and attitudes. They may reveal that they have had experiences similar to those of their client.

There is some disagreement among professional counselors as to the value of self-disclosure. Some professionals, psychoanalysts in particular, argue against all forms of self-disclosure. Others advocate it, contending that if counselees are to be helped, they need to know something about who their counselor really is so that a genuine relationship can develop. Psychiatrist Jerry Lewis offers sensible guidelines for those counselors who choose to reveal something of themselves:

1. The therapist can be genuine and be himself or herself in the course of psychotherapy without disclosing highly personal material.
2. The more personal the material the therapist considers disclosing, the greater the need to consider carefully the reasons for the proposed disclosure.
3. The more urgently the therapist feels a need to disclose, the greater the need to consider the reasons for the proposed disclosure.
4. The most common self-disclosure is to share one's feelings about a patient's communications. This provides interpersonal feedback regarding the patient's impact on others. It is particularly useful with patients whose difficulties include projecting their own thoughts and emotions onto others.
5. Certain patients who have a severe and chronic pathology and for whom treatment goals are limited may be helped by considerable self-disclosure by the therapist, if it is not highly personal. For some of these patients, the monthly or semi-monthly therapy sessions may represent rare moments of relief from alienation and loneliness.
6. When the therapist experiences intense feelings that cannot be hidden and the patient notes them, they should not be denied.
7. When considerably influenced by major events, the therapist's feelings may be disclosed.
8. Errors on the part of the therapist should be acknowledged.
9. No disclosure should be made without giving consideration to the most probable impact on the patient. [Lewis 1978, 88–89]

Two dangers in self-disclosure should be noted. First, self-disclosure tends to take the spotlight off the counselee and put it on the counselor. That can be very distracting to a troubled person. The client's sense of belonging may be seriously damaged if the counselor talks about himself or herself too much. Second, counselors may reveal material which will distort the relationship. For example, a counselor's self-disclosure may cause a client of the opposite sex to have romantic fantasies. Another possible hazard is that counselees may feel discouraged because they cannot live up to their idealized conception of what the counselor discloses. (I once disclosed to a client that I had gone through an experience similar to his; afterwards he berated himself for failing at something at which I had succeeded.)

In general, there should be self-disclosure only when a brief remark may underscore a common bond or mutual understanding. In many instances this affords an excellent opportunity to bring up Christian doctrine. By doctrinal self-disclosure, a counselor can introduce relevant Christian truths without interrupting the therapeutic flow.

Doctrinal self-disclosure does not mean reading from the Bible or wrenching the conversation from the subject at hand to interject a pious monologue. There is usually a natural place in the conversation to mention biblical concepts the counselor feels a client needs to understand for psychospiritual growth.

Counselors must avoid clichés and biblical jargon. Sermonic exhortations will not impress clients and will probably detract from the counselor's empathy. William Hulme observes that

> our challenge ... is to assist people in their movement from a superficial use of God-language to the genuine encounter that this language symbolizes. To do this we need to deal with God-talk symbols contextually—in the milieu of dialogue—rather than from any supposed authority of the counselor in such matters. [Hulme 1970, 42]

Note the contrast between Jesus and the self-styled religious authorities of His day, the scribes and Pharisees. "The people were amazed at his teaching, because he taught them as one who had authority, not as the teachers of the law" (Mark 1:22).

> In matters of faith any authority ... not accompanied by the authority of one's own involvement, tends to be authoritarian. In contrast the authority that comes from one's own involvement with God is by its very nature grounded in security. Therefore it can function within the flexibility that is needed for dialogue. [Hulme 1970, 42–43]

In other words, counselors must do more than know and recite the doctrine; they must actually live and be the doctrine. If doctrinal truths are an integral part of the counselor's own life, they will be a natural and unstrained part of the flow of conversation.

2. *Confrontation*

The second component of edification is confrontation. As counselor and counselee interact, the counselor will note various discrepancies and inconsistencies in the thoughts and actions of the client. Confrontation is "the bringing together of growth-defeating discrepancies in the client's perceptions, feelings, behavior, values, attitudes, and communication to compare and examine them" (Hammond 1977, 10). While no New Testament word is the exact equivalent of "confront," there are a number of closely related terms. They are variously translated "admonish," "reprove," "rebuke," "exhort," and "edify." In spite of their similarity there are subtle differences in their meanings. The point of interest for us is that they all signify speaking the truth "in such a way that it is acted upon by the one receiving it" (Hood 1979, 92).

In their book *Confrontation: For Better or for Worse* Bernard Berenson and Kevin Mitchell list five types of confrontation. Although there is overlap, we will deal with each of them separately:

a. *Didactic confrontation* involves giving counselees data they do not have or correcting misconceptions concerning relatively objective aspects of the world. In didactic confrontation a Christian therapist may impart doctrine to clients. It must be kept in mind that many clients are not looking for Bible teaching related to their problems. Whether one confronts with doctrine is a question to be decided by each counselor. If the one seeking help already understands the doctrine applicable to the particular situation, didactic confrontation is probably not necessary.

b. *Experiential confrontation* deals with various distortions and discrepancies occurring in or relating to the counselee's experience of himself:

1. Discrepancies between the client's expression of what he is and what he wants to be (actual self and idealized image of self).

154 The Essentials of Christian Counseling

2. Discrepancies between the client's abstract expressions about himself and his actual behavior as he himself reports it.
3. Discrepancies between the client's expressed experience of himself and the therapist's experience of him. [Patterson 1974, 76]

Distortions occur as an individual, unable to face reality, develops a twisted perception of it in order to fit personal needs. Various games, tricks, and smoke screens are used to hide the real self. One such defense mechanism is projection—attributing one's own undesirable emotions to someone else. For example, a person may come to believe that the suspicions and fears which he experiences are not really his, but the suspicions and fears of others, which cause them to be hostile to him. If such defense mechanisms prove successful in blotting out an unpleasant reality about oneself, the individual is likely to persist in using them. The counselor must exercise great caution in attempting to strip them away.

Christian therapists will encounter all sorts of inconsistencies in the lives of their clients. The proper course is either to suggest a different perspective, one from which the clients will be better able to face reality, or to challenge them to find more effective and rewarding ways of living (Egan 1977, 175–76). One very fruitful way of proceeding with certain Christians is to point out the discrepancy between their restored identity in Christ on one hand and their view of themselves on the other. Some counselees see themselves in a very unfavorable light because they do not fully understand who they really are in Christ.

c. *Strength confrontation* focuses on the assets and resources a counselee is utilizing only partially or not at all. Though strength confrontation has a negative element in that it points to a failure on the part of the client, the positive element is greater, for the emphasis is placed on what can be accomplished by utilizing one's strengths and assets.

d. *Weakness confrontation*, the opposite of strength confrontation, focuses on the counselee's deficiencies (Egan 1977, 178).

e. Finally, there is *encouragement to action*. The counselor urges the counselee to act constructively instead of remaining passive. The counselor will offer several suggestions for action (Egan 1977, 179–80).

As Christian therapists confront their clients, they will necessarily integrate their Christian faith into their counseling. What are we to say, then, in response to those who assert that therapists have no right to bring their personal values into the counseling arena? John Hoffman addresses this issue:

> I have argued that human existence always has a moral dimension, a reality only made more urgent by . . . the major social crises of our time. Any therapy therefore which seeks . . . to avoid a true ethical witness is bound to be inadequate because of its failure to equip counselees to function in the real world, a world of moral choices. *Moral confrontation is thus an ethical necessity.* [Hoffman 1979, 78, italics added]

We must also address the question of how to confront. Jay Adams has built his system of Christian therapy around "confronting another nouthetically" (from the Greek word *noutheteō*, meaning "to admonish"). Adams sees confrontation as the core of Christian counseling:

> Because nouthetic counseling seeks to correct sinful behavior patterns by personal confrontation and repentance, the stress is upon "What—what is wrong? and what needs to be done about it?" . . . *Nouthesis* is motivated by love and deep concern, in which clients are counseled and corrected by verbal means for their good, ultimately, of course, that God may be glorified. As Paul wrote in Colossians 1:28, every man must be confronted nouthetically in order that every man may be presented to Christ mature and complete. [Adams 1970, 49–50]

Great care must be exercised in all confrontation, since it is easy to take a "there you are" approach and thus to jeopardize the entire counseling relationship. Counselors must also guard against viewing confrontation as a verbal exchange, a game to be won by debate techniques. Such an exchange can "expose and defeat so that the confronter experiences triumph and the person confronted humiliation" (Carkhuff and Berenson 1977, 207–08). Proper confrontation, on the other hand, is characterized by empathy, tentativeness, and care (Egan 1977, 180–84). Counselors who display empathy, genuineness, respect, and concreteness of language tend to be more successful in confronting clients than do counselors lacking in these qualities. And their ability in this area tends to increase with time.

3. Immediacy

Immediacy in the interaction between therapist and client is the third essential component of edification. Since most emotional problems are closely tied in with and thus evidenced by poor interpersonal functioning, and since the way clients interact with their counselor is in general a reflection of how they interact with others in everyday life, it is to be expected that many of their difficulties will surface in the therapeutic relationship. "A good starting place to explore any client's ability to relate interpersonally is the client-counselor relationship itself." Gerard Egan speaks of "you-me" talk, the ability to discuss what is happening and how the counselee is feeling in the here and now (Egan 1975, 173).

The function of direct personal conversation is to enable those seeking help to receive immediate, ongoing, and expert feedback concerning how they relate to others.

> The way [the client] relates to the counselor is a snapshot of the way he relates to others. . . . Clients come to counseling manipulating, hostile, rejecting, testing. They invest or do not invest; they are afraid; they present weaknesses; they attempt to seduce; they stay in a shell; they hide; they try to force the counselor to be responsible; they try to force punishment from the counselor; they apologize for being human. If the counselor does not focus on trying to understand these things, growth possibilities for clients can be missed. [Patterson 1974, 84]

Advocating immediate interplay between counselor and counselee is in sharp opposition to the Freudian or analytic school, which views the counselor as a blank screen on which the counselee projects unresolved problems. Over a long period of time the counselee also redirects toward the counselor unhealthy thoughts and feelings which may have been unconsciously retained toward others since childhood. An analytic therapist allows this transference of thoughts and feelings to occur slowly and attempts to maintain a strict doctor-patient relationship. It must not be contaminated by direct personal interaction between counselor and counselee. With the therapist maintaining a distance, the focus is on the client's projections of unresolved thoughts and feelings.

The more active therapists advocate immediacy to bring the interpersonal element right to the fore. No doubt a certain amount of transference will occur and will have to be discussed and resolved. Immediacy, which involves the therapist as professional counselor, and not as a representative of some other important figure in the client's experience, helps to speed the process and enables the client to deal with unresolved problems swiftly. Direct encouragement of transference ("As you describe your fear of your mother, I wonder if perhaps you are experiencing similar feelings toward me right now") is an example of how a therapist advocating immediacy can speed the counseling process along.

Because immediacy of interaction has to do more with personal relationship between counselee and counselor than with the counselee's symptoms, it can produce added anxiety. Therefore we add a note of caution: being overly direct with a client can be harmful, probably more harmful than not being direct enough. To keep discussing "what's happening between us" soon loses its impact. In being direct the counselor must also be prepared for clients to question the value of the time spent together as well as the counselor's abilities and attributes. Such questions should be allowed and worked through.

The Goals of Christian Edification

The first goal of edification is for counselees to acquire fresh insight into the cause of their problems. Exploration of past relationships should bring insight into destructive patterns. Relational difficulties with the counselor can also be highly informative. From what happens in the counseling relationship effective counselors can deduce many of a client's basic emotional problems and detrimental past experiences.

The second goal is for counselees to work through their problems. Doctrinal self-disclosure by a Christian therapist can be of immense value here. By a brief, judiciously chosen and timed reference to a relevant doctrine, the counselor can be a channel for the biblical message. Gradually the scriptural teaching will be appropriated and internalized.

The counselor can also assist clients to work through their problems by helping them reconstruct the dynamics of past situations and past emotions. By direct discussion of a past incident which has harmful repercussions in the present or by playing the role of some other individual who figured prominently in it, the counselor can often induce the client to reexperience the emotions of that event. Or the counselor may simply make a general statement about the thoughts and feelings evoked by the incident. For example, "You must have felt hurt and humiliated when your father slapped you in front of your friends." A skilled counselor repeatedly assists clients to recollect, reconstruct, and reexperience events that have caused current problems. In reliving those events as it were, the counselee "undergoes literally hundreds of modifying learning experiences" (Colby 1951, 121). As the counselor confronts the client in this way, judiciously discloses doctrinal precepts, and strives for immediacy in the therapeutic relationship, the client will come to a better self-understanding and internalize biblical principles which will result in spiritual and emotional growth.

Service

The final stage in our model of Christian counseling is service (see Figure 23). Christians are called on to serve one another. The process of serving counselees culminates in bringing them to the point where they in turn can serve others. After a sense of belonging has given the counselee enough confidence to risk self-exploration and edification has led to internalization of biblical principles, externalization—moving out from one's own self and away from preoccupation with one's own needs—can take place. The goal of this stage of Christian counseling is effective living: the ability to handle the social and emotional dimensions of life. Self-destructive patterns will no longer hold sway; new spiritual resources will be discovered and utilized.

If there has been success in the earlier stages of the counseling process, the client will have been developing a personal course of action. This entails the hard work of finding ways to solve current

FIGURE 23   A Christian Model for Counseling—Stages 1, 2, and 3

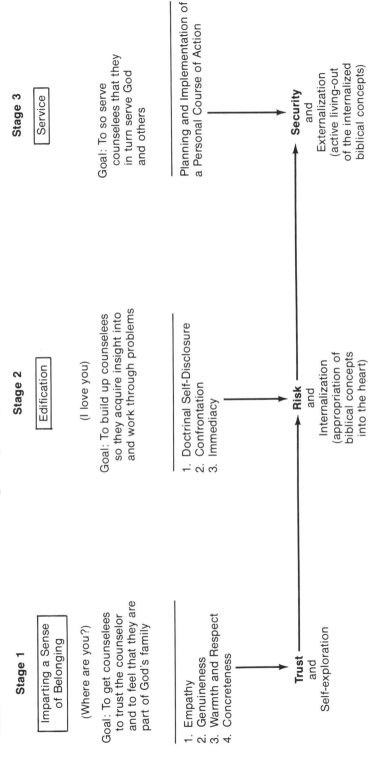

Stage 1

Imparting a Sense
of Belonging

(Where are you?)

Goal: To get counselees
to trust the counselor
and to feel that they are
part of God's family

1. Empathy
2. Genuineness
3. Warmth and Respect
4. Concreteness

Trust
and
Self-exploration

Stage 2

Edification

(I love you)

Goal: To build up counselees
so they acquire insight into
and work through problems

1. Doctrinal Self-Disclosure
2. Confrontation
3. Immediacy

Risk
and
Internalization
(appropriation of
biblical concepts
into the heart)

Stage 3

Service

Goal: To so serve
counselees that they
in turn serve God
and others

Planning and Implementation of
a Personal Course of Action

Security
and
Externalization
(active living-out
of the internalized
biblical concepts)

problems and even better methods for approaching future problems. A typical course of action will follow a general pattern:

1. The definition and description of the problem area(s).
2. The definition and description of directions and/or goals dictated by the problem area(s).
3. An analysis of the critical dimensions of these directions and/or goals.
4. A consideration of the alternative courses of action available for attaining the critical dimensions of these directions and/or goals.
5. A consideration of the advantages and disadvantages of the alternative courses of action.
6. The development of physical, emotional-interpersonal, and intellectual programs for following that course with the most advantages and fewest disadvantages in terms of ultimate achievement of the goals.
7. The development of progressive gradations of the programs involved. [Gazda 1973, 29]

The first three steps in this personal course of action should have been taken during the first two stages of counseling (self-exploration and internalization of biblical concepts). In those stages crucial interpersonal difficulties are resolved, debilitating feelings worked out, and obstacles to the appropriation of biblical truths removed.

Steps four through seven can be worked on during therapy sessions by asking questions such as, "Now that we see the problem, what can we do about it?" With a counselor's aid, counselees can explore the how, when, and where of options for action and service. It is important for the counselor to help counselees keep their plans realistic and workable. William Glasser comments, "Never make a plan that attempts too much, because it will usually fail and reinforce the already present failure. A failing person needs success, and he needs small individually successful steps to gain it" (Glasser 1972, 123).

After the working out of an appropriate plan, the counselor should elicit commitment to that plan from the counselee. There is a difficulty here in that "people with failure identities [are generally unwilling] to commit themselves, because in their loneliness they do not believe that anyone cares what they do" (Glasser 1972, 125–26). But the counselor's rapport with the counselee can motivate the counselee to follow through with the plan. Knowing that someone else really cares and is personally interested in seeing the plan implemented may be all that is needed. Even though this may create temporary dependence on the counselor, in the long run it will serve to build up the client's ego strength and independence.

Every Christian is called on to serve in the body of Christ. All Christians have been given specific talents and abilities to be used in mutual service. The counselor should stress activities which require cooperation with others, for a positive self-image and secure identity ultimately comes about only through relationships. If, as the client reaches the stage of serving others, the counselor feels that a certain biblical doctrine would be helpful, specific book titles or biblical passages should be suggested. To insure that the client follows through on the suggestion, the counselor might add that they will talk over the material together at the next session.

The climax of Christian counseling comes when the client begins to serve others. Having imparted a sense of belonging, the counselor earlier helped to engender within the client enough trust to begin the process of self-exploration. Edified and strengthened by the counselor, the client then risked further self-understanding, appropriated and internalized biblical concepts disclosed by the counselor, and worked through the most pressing problems. Now the process of serving the client has reached completion. For the client feels secure enough to externalize those biblical concepts in the service of others. The counseling program has been a success.

If there is a crucial factor running through the various steps of the counseling model outlined in these two chapters, it is the emphasis on mutuality, personal interaction, interdependence. The counselor and counselee must share themselves with each other. Indeed, Scripture makes it abundantly clear that being part of one another is an essential element of the Christian life. With this in mind, let us summarize once again our Christian model for counseling:

Stage 1. Imparting a sense of belonging

1. **Empathy.** "We . . . are . . . every one members one of another" (Rom. 12:5, King James)

    love one another
    accept one another
    care for one another
    be devoted to one another
    show forbearance to one another
    be hospitable to one another

2. **Genuineness.** "Do not lie to each other" (Col. 3:9)

    be subject to one another
    give preference to one another
    clothe yourselves with humility toward one another
    confess your faults to one another

3. **Warmth.** "Be devoted to one another in brotherly love. Honor one another above yourselves" (Rom. 12:10)

    increase and abound in love for one another
    forgive each other
    let us not judge one another

4. **Concreteness**

Stage 2. Edification

1. **Doctrinal self-disclosure.** "Encourage one another and build each other up" (1 Thess. 5:11)

    speak to one another in psalms and hymns
    teach and admonish one another
    pursue the things which make for peace for the building up of one another

2. **Confrontation.** "Admonish one another" (Rom. 15:14, King James)

    teach and admonish one another
    do not speak against one another

3. **Immediacy.** "Have sincere love for your brothers, love one another deeply, with all your hearts" (1 Peter 1:22)

Stage 3. Service. "Serve one another in love" (Gal. 5:13)

    care for one another
    bear with one another
    stimulate one another to love and good deeds
    bear one another's burdens
    pray for one another

8

Diagnosis
Type of Personality and Idealized Image

The Importance of Investigating the Early Years

The writers of Scripture were very much aware that what we learn as children has an overriding influence on the rest of our lives. Accordingly, they continually underscored the necessity of training children spiritually and psychologically. "Train a child in the way he should go, and when he is old he will not turn from it" (Prov. 22:6). "He who spares the rod hates his son, but he who loves him is careful to discipline him" (Prov. 13:24). Paul enjoined, "Fathers, do not embitter your children, or they will become discouraged" (Col. 3:21). In other words, we must not be overly severe, nag, or do anything else which will cause our children to lose heart or feel inferior. Paul also spoke highly of the godly upbringing Timothy had received from his mother and grandmother (2 Tim. 1:5). Of course, the supreme biblical teaching on parenting is God's fathering of His own people. He is the model parent to be emulated.

The attitudes that children absorb from their parents will stay with them throughout life. That early learning, it has been said, has a hundred times more power than does what we later learn as adults. Since the Bible and psychological research both emphasize that how one develops in childhood is a basic cause of later personality and behavioral traits, a counselor should be fully informed about a client's early environment. Was the home atmosphere warm, loving, and accepting, or cold, punitive, and rejecting? It is essential that the counselor be aware of the unique factors which have contributed to the counselee's present problems. It is possible that these factors may not be exclusively environmental in nature. There may also be organic factors, including genetically transmitted tendencies such as a predisposition to schizophrenia, depression, or some other major affective (mood) disorder (see Figure 24). Understanding the unique factors will help the Christian counselor, guided by the Holy Spirit, discern which doctrines should become an integral part of the counseling process so that the client may internalize and apply them.

The reason for exploring the past is not to place blame but to produce understanding. It has been said that

> yesterday's hurt
> is today's understanding
> rewoven into tomorrow's love.

The ultimate reason for exploring the past, then, is to produce love, which is the goal of all Christian counseling. We need not fear that the client's interpersonal functioning will be hindered by this process, for nothing will surface which is not already there.

FIGURE 24   Developmental Factors Affecting Personality

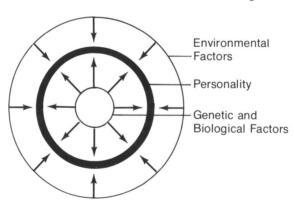

Environmental Factors

Personality

Genetic and Biological Factors

It is ironic that while the church eagerly proclaims that Christian character is produced by positive home influences, at the same time it stubbornly resists the notion that past influences may explain negative personality traits in adults. We cannot logically accept the one concept without the other. This does not mean, however, that counselors should pursue a client's past to the extent Sigmund Freud advocated—delving into each stage in the development of the libido (oral, anal, phallic, and genital) with all the attendant traumas and fixations. Rather, like psychoanalyst Karen Horney, we should focus on the general directions of an individual's history.

Freud maintained that detailed investigation of the development of an individual's libido is crucial to the psychoanalytic process; he stressed the concept of "repetition compulsion," the theory that we are subconsciously driven to repeat infantilisms in the hope of re-creating the pleasure that such behavior once engendered. Horney disagreed (Horney 1939, 209). She believed that "genetic understanding [investigation of libidinal development] is useful only as long as it helps the functional understanding" (Horney 1937, 33). In other words, she viewed exploring an individual's development as a means of understanding the general flow of the river of his life. She was interested in the important persons and influences along the way, not in every rock and waterfall that was encountered. She regarded the interpersonal and social dimensions of life as primary:

> There is no doubt whatever that childhood experiences exert a decisive influence on development and, as I have said, it is one of Freud's many merits to have seen this in greater detail and with more accuracy than before. ... In my opinion the influence (of childhood) operates in two ways. One is that it leaves traces which can be directly traced. A spontaneous like or dislike of a person may have to do directly with early memories of similar traits in father, mother, siblings. ... Adverse experiences ... will make a child lose at an early age his spontaneous trust in the benevolence and justice of others. Also he will lose or never acquire a naive certainty of being wanted. In this sense of, let us say, anticipating evil rather than good, the old experiences enter directly into adult ones.
>
>   The other and more important [influence] is that the sum total of childhood experiences brings about a certain character structure,

or rather starts its development. With some persons this development essentially stops at the age of five. With some it stops in adolescence, with others at around thirty, with a few it goes on until old age. . . . The past in some way or other is always contained in the present. [Horney 1939, 152–53]

To emphasize the sum total of childhood experiences, however, is not to imply that it is wrong to try to trace certain problems to particular stages in an individual's development. For if parents mishandle a crucial period in their child's life (especially the period of an infant's individuation from its mother and the period of puberty and adolescence), emotional growth can be arrested. And indeed, an exceptionally traumatic event, such as the early loss of a parent, may so upset the child as to produce severe negative results in adulthood.

Nevertheless, Horney's main focus is on the overall interpersonal dimensions of the individual's early years. Relationships with one's parents are of particular importance. She submits a long list of factors which can result in problems in adulthood:

Overdomination by parents, indifference, erratic treatment, lack of respect for the child's individual needs, lack of real guidance, disparaging attitude, too much admiration (or its absence), lack of encouragement and warmth from parents, too much (or too little) responsibility, overprotection, isolation [of parents] from their children, injustice, discrimination, unkept promises, hostile atmosphere, quarrelsome parents and so on and so on. These factors leave a child feeling insecure and basically anxious, "helpless in a potentially hostile world." [Horney 1945, 41]

We saw in chapter 4 that every human being has certain basic needs—a sense of belonging, self-esteem, and control (strength). Parents can to a limited extent fulfill their children's needs. But if there are major difficulties in the parent-child relationship, those needs go totally unfulfilled and will consequently be exaggerated in later life.

We saw in chapter 5 that the basic needs of the mature individual can be satisfied through God's work of restoring the human identity. But if in the past an individual's needs have not been at least partially met by his or her parents, certain emotional difficulties will have developed which will prove to be obstacles to realizing God's work of restoring the human heart (see Figure 25; cf. Figure 15, p. 102). If parents, for example, fail to impart a sense of belonging, of acceptance, but instead show little care and concern, in effect rejecting the child, the child will be anxious and insecure. If, in addition, parents display a resentment toward the child instead of love and affection, anger ("I am angry at my parents for not showing me the love other parents show to their children"—this hostility may later extend to the whole world) and guilt ("What's wrong with me?") will be added to the anxiety. The individual will have little or no grounds for self-esteem. And if, instead of affirming the child's worth, thus imparting strength and confidence, parents also ridicule and shame the child, depression and an exaggerated need for control will be the result.

Anxiety, insecurity, anger, guilt, depression—an individual in whom these emotional difficulties are severe has exaggerated needs for a sense of belonging, self-esteem, and control. But those very emotional difficulties will keep the troubled individual from an awareness of God's restorative work: the Father's adoption of human beings into His family, which gives a sense of belonging; the Son's love, which builds self-esteem; the Holy Spirit's empowering of the redeemed individual with strength and control. Therefore, it is vital that the nature of the emotional problems be identified, understood, and worked through. Their causes will be found be examining the history of the counselee's interpersonal relationships within the family, at school, and among peers.

Marshall Hodge notes that the negative feelings children develop as a result of poor relationships with their parents build on each other:

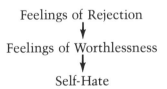

"The most significant people in my life—that is, my parents—do not appear to consider me to be of personal worth; therefore I must be worthless." As that kind of thinking persists and intensifies, the child's internal logic leads to self-hate and often to a lack of confidence, strength, and control. "I seem to be worth-

FIGURE 25   Obstacles to Realization of God's Work
             of Restoring Human Identity

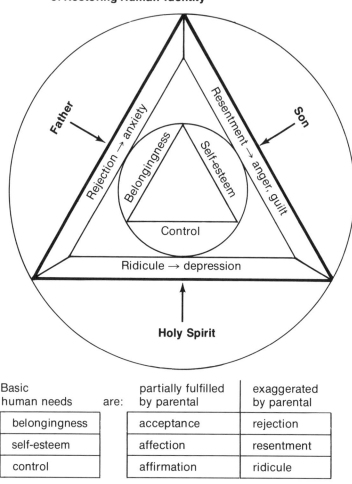

Basic human needs	are:	partially fulfilled by parental	exaggerated by parental
belongingness		acceptance	rejection
self-esteem		affection	resentment
control		affirmation	ridicule

less. I appear inferior to my parents and other people around me.
I cannot respect myself, since they don't seem to respect me.
Since I am worthless, I hate myself" (Hodge 1967, 25).

Through sensitive discussion with the client the counselor can
determine whether and to what extent the "three R's"—rejection, resentment, and ridicule—were present in the family background. The findings (e.g., whether the parents were totally
rejecting, partially rejecting, or accepting) can then be plotted on

a continuum (see Figure 26). The person who was subject to parental rejection, resentment, and/or ridicule will have exaggerated needs, respectively, for a sense of belonging, self-esteem, and/or control. Each area needs to be examined to determine its role in preventing wholeness.

FIGURE 26   A Chart for Plotting the "Three R's"

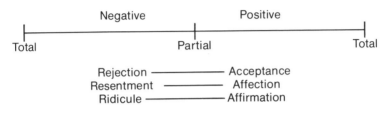

Exaggerated Needs as the Determinant of Personality

Karen Horney sees a general pattern in the way a child copes with basic needs which become exaggerated because of parental rejection, resentment, or ridicule:

1. The child is subjected to a stressful environment which produces basic anxiety.
2. A strategy is developed to cope with the stress.
3. Because the strategy reduces anxiety, it becomes highly significant for the individual.
4. The strategy may be elevated to the status of a general orientation to life. It becomes compulsive and is indiscriminately used. [cited in DiCaprio 1974, 313]

The need for a sense of belonging, self-esteem, or control can become so strong that it determines the basic orientation a person has toward others and toward the world in general. Thus it can actually become the prime determinant of personality.

An Exaggerated Need to Belong—
The Self-Effacing Personality

Overt or covert rejection prevents children from feeling that they belong. An exaggerated need to belong results. Horney notes that there are two fundamental manifestations of this need:

1. "The neurotic need for affection and approval." This is an indiscriminate need to please others, to be liked and favorably regarded by them. Pleasing others is seen as the way to win love.
2. "The neurotic need for a 'partner' who will take over one's life." Of this need Horney says, "The center of gravity is entirely in the 'partner' who is to fulfill all expectations of life and take responsibility for good and evil." [Horney 1942, 54–55]

These two manifestations of an exaggerated need to belong combine to form what Horney calls the "moving toward [others]" or self-effacing personality. She observes that "however these needs may vary in their expression, they ... center around a desire for human intimacy, a desire for 'belonging.' " Self-effacing individuals regard love as the answer to their underlying insecurities. The way they deal with others seems to be built on the premise, "If you love me, you won't hurt me." Thus the "moving toward" personality feels compelled to be self-sacrificing, compliant, sympathetic, and dependent. (Rubins 1972, 151).

Horney lists three characteristics of the self-effacing person: a feeling of being weak and helpless; a tendency to subordinate oneself, remaining submissive and compliant while allowing someone else to control and dominate; and a general dependence on others (usually one person in particular). The self-effacing person clings to another for nurture and emotional input that will provide a sense of identity (in reality the sense of identity comes from being an appendage to the partner or stronger person) (Horney 1945, 48–81). "In summary, this type needs to be liked, wanted, desired, loved; to feel accepted, welcomed, approved of, appreciated; to be needed, to be of importance to others, especially to one particular person; to be helped, protected, taken care of, guided" (Horney 1945, 5).

Dominick Barbara has sketched an extreme example of the self-effacing personality:

Behavioristically we refer to these extremes, these compulsive expressions of compliancy, timidity and dependent needs in individuals, as the process of self-effacement. This self-effacing person ... will go out of his way to subordinate himself to others, to be dependent on them, to strive to serve them. And if singled out for special attention he will be uneasy. In relation to himself, our timid speaker lives with a diffuse sense of failure because of his inability to be liked and admired as he feels he should be. In a passive way he judges himself guilty, inferior, beneath notice. He is afraid to express such expansive qualities as self-glorification or arrogance, and self-pride is strictly taboo. He will suppress in himself any reaction that might seem to signify ambition, vindictiveness or a seeking after his own advantage.

We see self-effacement as a way of life highlighted today in such well-known characters as Mr. Peepers, The Timid Soul, or Mr. Milk Toast. In each, the personality is portrayed in terms of a clumsy, childlike, fearful, confused, naive soul, prey for all who would take advantage of him, the butt of jokes and pranks—in a broad sense one who is crippled by inhibitions and taboos. Yet we usually respond to them with pity, sympathy and loving affection, and a sense of identification with their victimized and underdog existences. Actually we are prone to make virtues of the self-effacing person's neurotic attitudes, his Pollyanna viewpoint so easily confused with a genuine faith in the goodness of mankind, his pseudogoodness, his forced generosity, his sense of stoic nobility and his conscious air of suffering and self-inflicted martyrdom. [Barbara 1958, 77–78]

An Exaggerated Need for Self-Esteem— The Expansive Personality

Children who do not receive love and affection fail to develop a sense of self-esteem. An exaggerated need for self-esteem results. Horney notes five ways in which the need manifests itself:

1. "The neurotic need for power." There is a craving for power for the purpose of subordinating and dominating others. Strength is glorified; weakness is despised. One may try to control others either through foresight and superior reasoning, or by force of the will.
2. "The neurotic need to exploit others and by hook or crook get the better of them." An unloved child will later use other people strictly for his or her own gain.
3. "The neurotic need for social recognition or prestige." There is a determined effort to gain public attention and accep-

tance. Other people are judged by their competitiveness and ability to win recognition.

4. "The neurotic need for personal admiration." Individuals who were deprived of affection in their childhood may compensate by developing an inflated picture of themselves, an idealized image, and need to have that image reinforced by the admiration of others.

5. "The neurotic need for personal achievement." Individuals who were resented by their parents may feel the need to surpass others in all activities. They want and strive to be the very best in all pursuits. [Horney 1942, 55–58]

These five manifestations of an exaggerated need for self-esteem combine to form what Horney calls the "moving against [others]" or expansive personality. Persons with an expansive personality take it for granted that everyone else is hostile. They operate on the premise, "If I have power, no one can hurt me." To glorify themselves they must dominate others. Although the "moving against" personality may present an attractive façade and use all the right words, he or she is simply manipulating and exploiting others to gain control.

> The expansive solution requires mastery over life and over others in the neurotic sense of domination and self-glorification. Certain personality traits have positive values for such an individual. These include hardness, strength, efficiency, domination, aggression, shrewdness, ambition . . . success, and insensitivity to the feelings of others. He needs to control, have his way, complete and outdo, and gain prestige. He shuns affection, sympathy, and trust as weakness; he is afraid to admit to error or imperfection, even illness, for these represent negative values. He sees himself without limits, confident and superior. He mistrusts others and sees them as potential competitors. [Rubins 1972, 151]

Like the "moving toward" personality, the "moving against" personality is also attempting to deal with underlying anxiety and insecurity. It is imperative to control others through assertiveness and aggression. For by controlling others one can ward off the fear of being hurt or humiliated by them.

Psychiatrist Barbara paints as vivid a picture of the expansive personality as he did of the self-effacing personality:

[The expansive personality] uses such familiar clichés as "He who hesitates is lost" and also "A sucker is a person who lets someone else get the best of him." Since his one chief orientation in life is the attainment of prestige and success, he shies away from any resemblance to softer feelings for either himself or others. He finds he has little time to concern himself with the frailties of living. His major concern is with what he will get out of any given situation and "never mind how others feel about it." At times his ambitious struggle for success becomes so compulsive and driven that he will push himself to any extremes in order to keep his physical self functioning like a well-oiled machine. Because he uses his work only as a means to an end and not for any form of self-satisfaction, he rarely enjoys what he does in spite of the tremendous energy he puts forth in the doing.

In placing a premium on such qualities as toughness, hardness, invulnerability, shrewdness, cynicism and machine-like efficiency, the aggressive man or woman feels justified in acting disparagingly and exploitively toward other people. But while he may give the appearance of being uninhibited, overly assertive and in command of most situations, he actually has as many inhibitions as the compliant neurotic. He may consider the gentler emotions such as love, affection, generosity as sloppy sentimentality, yet deep inside him he is highly sensitive to rebuff, rejection and criticism and craves to be liked by his fellows. However, his own greatest fear is that he will be thought soft and will become so and will therefore be taken advantage of and exploited. He is psychologically compelled to maintain his own wall of armor. [Barbara 1958, 85–86]

An Exaggerated Need for Control— The Resigned Personality

Children who are ridiculed and shamed by their parents will lack strength and confidence. Consequently, they have an exaggerated need for control. This need manifests itself in three ways:

1. "The neurotic need for self-sufficiency and independence." Individuals whose worth was never attested by parental affirmation will endeavor to prove that they are dependent on nothing and no one. They will yield to no influence; they will avoid becoming close to others. Maintaining one's distance and separateness is the only real source of security.

2. "The neurotic need for perfection and unassailability." A relentless driving for superiority will result in the feeling that one actually is superior, the impression that one is perfect and infallible.
3. "The neurotic need to restrict one's life within narrow borders; the necessity to be undemanding and contented with little and to restrict ambitions and wishes for material things." People who feel they have little control over life and themselves tend to be ultrareactionary and conservative, and to retire to the background. [Horney 1942, 59–60]

These three manifestations of an exaggerated need for control combine to form what Horney calls the "moving away [from others]" or resigned personality. The resigned personality strives to avoid all emotion and operates on the premise, "If I withdraw, nothing can hurt me."

The traits of resignation are mostly negative—aloofness, reduction of material wants, detachment. The individual's needs are for privacy, not to compete, not to be involved or committed; he wants to be self-sufficient and independent. He fears influence, obligation, intrusion, coercion, pressure, change, which he may feel to emanate from others, even if this feeling is without foundation. His need for detachment renders emotional ties intolerable; anticipated closeness through sex and marriage may cause anxiety. All awareness of such attitudes as love or aggression is inhibited. [Rubins 1972, 152]

The "moving away" personality builds an emotional fort in which he or she lives alone. Retreating behind huge emotional walls that shut others out, such an individual communicates only by yelling over the tops of those walls. The resigned personality can never be coaxed out of the security of the fortress. Life in the fort, though lonely, gives one a feeling of being unassailable, invulnerable, and superior to others. The detachment inherent in such a lifestyle allows that feeling to go unchallenged, thus reinforcing the sense of safety.

Close ties with others are of course impossible for resigned personalities. And the attitude which they take toward themselves might best be categorized as benumbed objectivity. Their unconscious attempts to deal with the emptiness, loneliness, and eventual despair which they suffer usually take one of three forms: a persistent resignation, with an aversion to all kinds of activity; a passive resistance to societal restrictions which might itself someday erupt into active rebellion; or an extremely shallow life-style characterized by constant activity, including indiscriminate sex, superficial social relations, and participation in all manner of causes (Rubins 1972, 152).

Dominick Barbara draws us still another portrait, this time an extreme example of the resigned personality:

> The neurotic belonging to this group avoids, if he can, conflicting situations and strives to settle for "peace at any price." Driven by his fear of the potential threat of inter-relationship, he resigns himself to becoming an onlooker—both at himself and at the world in which he moves. This of necessity restricts all the vital areas of his life.
>
> Unable to face himself in a realistic sense, this "man of few words" represses or denies many of his real feelings and desires by placing inhibitions and checks on their expression, and at the same time he will minimize or flatly deny his real assets or potentialities. It is his aversion toward making realistic sacrifices in order to achieve his life goals that induces him to give up the struggle and resign himself to what he thinks of as a peaceful position. This attitude he rationalizes by saying in effect that the issue just isn't worth the effort or that life is too short to worry about it. He will choose a vocation, a partner in marriage, friends—provided these will not interfere with an existence which permits him to remain to some degree self-sufficient and apart. In this self-imposed confinement, he avoids healthy competitiveness and holds himself to a minimum. [Barbara 1958, 103–04]

Each of the three major types of personality we have described develops its own powerful style, which is in effect an attempt to deal with the often insatiable need which created it. The self-effacing ("moving toward") personality is driven by an excessive need to belong, the expansive ("moving against") personality by an exaggerated need for self-esteem, the resigned ("moving away") personality by an inordinate need for competence, strength, and control. Christians as well as non-Christians usually find one of the three patterns dominant in their life. If the pattern becomes overwhelming, preventing one from normal human functioning, it must be dealt with thoroughly.

The Divided Self and the Three Major Types of Personality

We observed in chapter 4 (pp. 83–85) that as a consequence of the fall Adam's unified self or ego was split into (1) a needing self and (2) a rejected self. This division lies at the core of all psychospiritual disorders. In addition, it is to be noted that there is a correlation between personality type and the relative strength of the two parts of the divided self.

1. The needing self is already evident at birth. Every infant has an intense need for care and affection. Hundreds of studies have documented the severe damage which occurs when an infant is deprived of its mother or for some other reason receives little or no love during the early months of life. While the demands which the needing self makes are especially powerful during the first two years, they will continue throughout life. The human personality always needs love, affection, nurture, affirmation, and approval. Without proper nurture the needing self starves, and the emotional effects are devastating.

Adults whose needing self has been undernourished will try to compensate in infantile ways. For example, love-starved persons may search for a substitute parent to fill their needs. A chronic dependence on others may well result. If feelings of weakness and helplessness are also present, this dependence will inevitably increase. Compulsive and indiscriminate sexual behavior is another way of seeking to fulfill the need for love and intimacy. I am reminded here of a student at a Christian college whose love needs were of such abnormal proportions that, without any financial motivation whatsoever, she would go out at night as a prostitute. She did not stop to consider that such relationships would not only be inadequate to fulfill her need for love but would be destructive as well. (It should be stressed that "physical sexual symptoms mask a more broadly based and significant need for personal relationship in its basic security-giving value" [Guntrip 1971, 168]. This holds true for all types of sexual behavior, including deviant forms such as homosexuality. When sex is an integral part of a warm, personal, moral relationship, it can be a mature fulfillment of the needing self.) Another immature way of trying to compensate for lack of affection is to seek love without giving any in return. Some people try to possess another totally but dare not risk sharing themselves in the process. Their only concern is their own personal fulfillment.

2. The problems presented by the rejected self are intensified by parents who perpetually criticize, demonstrate hostility, and in general withhold their approval. Such parents in effect abandon their child emotionally. As a result, the child experiences frustration, anger, anxiety, depression, and often a sense of helplessness. Feelings of inferiority, incompetence, and inadequacy become deeply engrained.

Such children accept and identify with the rejecting messages they receive. They see themselves as the unlovable person they are told they are. Once that happens, the rejected self becomes the rejecting self as well. That is, rejected individuals will begin to torture, persecute, and hate themselves. Continued rejection not only by others but by oneself as well increases the feelings of anger and depression. Once activated the rejecting ego has great destructive power. On an unconscious level basic feelings of worthlessness are created: "I'm so bad that I don't deserve to be loved by anyone good; I don't deserve to succeed; no decent person would want me; of what value am I?" This process of self-rejection, which is a prevalent clinical pattern, prevents its victims from responding to others and, worse yet, to the unconditional love of Christ.

In some individuals the needing self predominates; in others, the rejected/rejecting self. A debilitating anxiety arises in both cases, but especially in the latter. As a general rule, there is a correlation between which part of the divided self predominates and personality type (see Figure 27):

1. An individual in whom the needing self is dominant will tend to be a "moving toward" type of personality. There will be a desperate attempt to comply, to conform, in order to satisfy unmet needs for love and affection.
2. An individual in whom the rejected/rejecting self is dominant will tend to be a "moving against" personality. Since the tender emotions of the needing self are subordinate, the individual will make little effort to fulfill natural needs in

a mature way. Instead of trust and love there will be negativism and hostility, fear and guilt. There will be a continual persecution and torturing of the self.

3. An individual in whom both the needing self and the rejected/rejecting self are unbearably strong, but neither is dominant, will tend to be a "moving away" personality. The pain and fear experienced by the needing and rejected/rejecting selves are so excruciating that detachment from the rest of the world seems to be the only solution.

FIGURE 27   The Divided Self and Personality Type

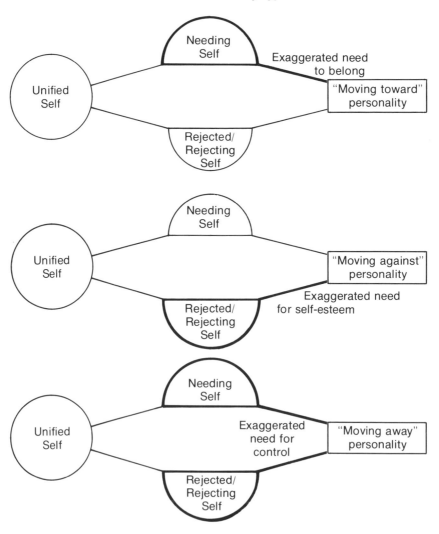

Our split egos constitute the basic core or "real self" of our personality. The balance between the needing self and the rejected/rejecting self helps determine the particular style each individual will adopt in coping with life. Awareness of the status of the two parts of the divided self generally enables a counselor to detect a troubled person's inner world and perception of reality. If there is a deep self-hatred or a strong feeling of helplessness, living with one's real self becomes unbearable. Individuals who are unable to accept themselves will feel they are unacceptable to others also. To escape from depression and anxiety, such persons move away from their intolerable real self toward an idealized image, a false self.

The Idealized Image

To deal with feelings of insecurity, we develop an idealized image of ourselves. This is basically what was in view when Freud spoke of the "ego ideal" and Alfred Adler spoke of our striving for superiority to compensate for feelings of inferiority. It was Horney, however, who most clearly expounded the concept of the idealized image: when living with one's real self becomes too painful, the mind postulates a false self. This idealized image is an escape that betrays a basic self-hatred or nonacceptance of self. Initially, one is conscious that the idealized image is a fantasy, as when a girl envisions herself as a beautiful princess living in a huge castle with a handsome prince, or a boy pictures himself scoring the winning touchdown or home run. But later, as the image is embellished, the individual gradually comes to identify with it. The individual clings to this glorified self-portrait because it relieves anxiety, satisfies exaggerated needs, and represents the negative qualities of the real self as glorious ideals instead. For example, the compliance and submission of a "moving toward" personality come to be viewed as goodness, love, saintliness, and service. The assertiveness and aggression of a "moving against" personality come to be viewed as strength, heroism, leadership, and power. And the aloofness of a "moving away" personality is interpreted to be wisdom, self-control, and independence.

As time passes, the real self is abandoned in favor of the idealized image. All of one's energies go into actualizing and maintaining the image. Horney warns us that this idealized image is a representation of perfection and as such is never attainable. She laments the abandonment of the real self for the idealized image, which she labels "a devouring monster."

> Surveying self-hate and its ravaging force, we cannot help but see in it a great tragedy, perhaps the greatest of the human mind. Man in reaching out for the Infinite and Absolute also starts destroying himself. When he makes a pact with the devil, who promises him glory, he has to go to hell—to the hell within himself. [Horney 1950, 154]

Horney directs our attention to Christ's successful resistance of Satan's promise to give the kingdoms of the world in exchange for obeisance. Jesus did not abandon His real self (i.e., He did not deny His deity by bowing to Satan) for the sake of the idealized image (ruler over the kingdoms of the world) with which Satan tried to seduce Him. Resisting temptation of this nature is a sign of true greatness (Horney 1950, 375). Horney calls the struggle to actualize one's idealized image "the devil's pact" since it costs the individual so dearly in alienation from the real self.

In the struggle to attain the idealized image at least three unhealthy personality traits are evident: (1) overdriving ambition, (2) perfectionism, and (3) anger (see Figure 28). Overdriving, neurotic ambition sets goals for the self which are beyond reach. Being good is not enough; one has to be great or the best. No matter what the cost, one must excel. The individual is under constant intense pressure to live up to the demands of these unattainable goals, which, of course, require perfection. It is not enough to do something well; it must be done perfectly. Then too there is anger or frustration with whoever or whatever has supposedly hindered the individual from attaining these goals. Since it is impossible to live up to the ideal and one can no longer blame the real self (it has been disowned), the individual turns to what is imagined to be the obstacle. Others receive the full force of blame, wrath, and, if possible, humiliation.

There are certain other elements which are necessarily involved as one endeavors to attain the idealized image. First, to avoid having to look at the real self, a certain amount of false pride must be maintained. The individual can then begin to iden-

FIGURE 28   The Struggle to Attain the Idealized Self

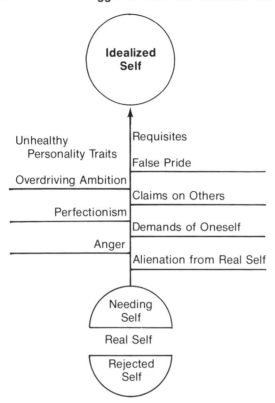

tify with the glories of the image instead of with the shortcomings of the real self. Self-love, narcissism, and delusions of greatness and grandeur result. (Do not forget that pride is basically resistance to God and the cause of the fall of the human race.) False pride induces the individual to view his or her weaknesses and faults as virtues. For example, as we have seen, submission may come to be regarded as saintliness.

Second, people struggling to attain their idealized image make claims on others. Narcissistic personalities believe they have special rights and privileges. They may, for example, feel that it is their right, their due, to be honored, to be loved, never to be disagreed with or criticized. They may act as if they were omnipotent and Godlike. All of us have seen leaders in the fields of religion and politics who act as if they were above criticism.

Third, people struggling to achieve their idealized images also make impossible demands of themselves. Projecting an image of perfection, of Godlikeness, puts one under a consuming lifelong bondage. We might call this the "tyranny of the shoulds"—"I should be this; I ought to do that."

Finally, there is an ever growing alienation from oneself. The farther one gets from the despised real self, the better. And the more grandiose the image, the farther away one can get. However, like all the other requisite ingredients in the struggle to attain the idealized image—false pride, inordinate claims on others, impossible demands of oneself—alienation from self is tragic from a psychological standpoint and sinful from a biblical standpoint.

Jesus was well aware that the struggle to achieve the idealized image is both tragic and sinful. In the Sermon on the Mount He emphasized that attainment of the idealized image (the righteousness of the Pharisees), even if feasible, would be insufficient for salvation:

> For I tell you that unless your righteousness surpasses that of the Pharisees and the teachers of the law, you will certainly not enter the kingdom of heaven.
>
> You have heard that it was said to the people long ago, "Do not murder, and anyone who murders will be subject to judgment." But I tell you that anyone who is angry with his brother will be subject to judgment. . . .
>
> You have heard that it was said, "Do not commit adultery." But I tell you that anyone who looks at a woman lustfully has already committed adultery with her in his heart. [Matt. 5:20–22, 27–28]

Six times in Matthew 5 (vv. 21, 27, 31, 33, 38, 43) we read, "You have heard that it was said. . . . But I tell you. . . ." Now Jesus had no quarrel with what Moses had enjoined ("Do not think that I have come to abolish the Law or the Prophets; I have not come to abolish them but to fulfill them," v. 17). Rather His dispute was with the Pharisees, who had distorted the teaching of Moses. In their view righteousness was a matter of ritual, rules, and regulations. Spiritual status was achieved by living up to the ideal of fulfilling every detail of the law. By contrast Jesus stressed the spirit rather than the letter of the law, and the real self rather than the idealized image. Jesus in effect told the Pharisees that God will never accept us on the basis of our struggle to achieve the idealized image, since that struggle necessarily involves false pride, alienation from self and God, and hypocrisy (for Jesus' warnings against hypocrisy see, e.g., Matt. 6:2, 5, 16).

All of us are guilty of trying to cover up and hide from our real selves. We desperately want others to think that we are like our idealized image. A. W. Tozer notes this as he comments on Matthew 5:5 ("Blessed are the meek, for they will inherit the earth"):

> [The meek] will get deliverance from the burden of pretense . . . the common desire to put the best foot forward and hide from the world our real inward poverty. . . . There is hardly a man or woman who dares to be just what he or she is without doctoring up the impression. The fear of being found out gnaws like rodents within their hearts. . . . Let no one smile this off. These burdens are real, and little by little they kill the victims of this evil and unnatural way of life. And the psychology created by years of this kind of thing makes true meekness seem as unreal as a dream, as aloof as a star. [Tozer 1955, 114]

Even the apostles were plagued with delusions that they could attain their idealized image. For example, they argued on several occasions about which one of them would be greatest in the kingdom of heaven. Peter made statements which he honestly believed, but which reflected his idealized image rather than his real self. Although he pledged to Jesus, "Even if all fall away on account of you, I never will" (Matt. 26:33), and "Lord, I am ready to go with you to prison or to death" (Luke 22:33), he was unable to keep his promise.

Delusions regarding the attainability and efficacy of the idealized image had also plagued the apostle Paul:

> Watch out for those dogs, those men who do evil, those mutilators of the flesh. For it is we who are the circumcision, we who worship by the Spirit of God, who glory in Christ Jesus, and who put no confidence in the flesh—though I myself have reasons for such confidence.
>
> If anyone else thinks he has reasons to put confidence in the flesh, I have more: circumcised on the eighth day, of the people of Israel, of the tribe of Benjamin, a Hebrew of Hebrews; in regard to the law, a Pharisee; as for zeal, persecuting the church; as for legalistic righteousness, faultless.
>
> But whatever was to my profit I now consider loss for the sake

of Christ. What is more, I consider everything a loss compared to the surpassing greatness of knowing Christ Jesus my Lord, for whose sake I have lost all things. I consider them rubbish, that I may gain Christ and be found in him, not having a righteousness of my own that comes from the law, but that which is through faith in Christ—the righteousness that comes from God and is by faith. [Phil. 3:2–9]

Paul is here explaining his former reliance on the aspirations and achievements of the idealized self ("a Hebrew of Hebrews") and his subsequent abandonment of that reliance so that he could be his real self, the only self with which Christ deals. The same theme is to be found in 2 Corinthians 11:21–12:10. After listing a catalogue of personal experiences and accomplishments which one might be tempted to boast about, Paul notes that God sent him a thorn in the flesh to keep him from becoming conceited. The chief passage on Paul's struggle to achieve his idealized image, however, is Romans 7, where he talks about his inability to live up to the Pharisaic laws.

There is a perennial struggle between one's idealized image (false self) and one's real self. Christian therapy must elicit the real self, no matter how hated and despised it might be, rather than encourage attempts to actualize the idealized image. It is the real self which Christ loves and accepts. Paul abandoned his struggle to attain the idealized image and faced who he really was (both his needing and rejected/rejecting self). At that point he came to understand that Christ loves and accepts the real self and can fulfill its needs. In Christ our real self becomes our "true" self (see Figure 29). While the real self and the true self are actually the same, they are differentiated here to stress that the real self, which experiences great needs and an excessive amount of rejection, can find fulfillment and acceptance in Christ and in Him alone. Assured of His acceptance, we can become our true selves. In Him we have a basis for restored identity, a positive self-image, and self-esteem. Of primary importance is the total reversal of the pathologic, sinful flow described earlier. No longer do we abandon the real self in quest of a false, idealized self. Instead, in Christ we come to accept our real self and begin to move toward our true self.

FIGURE 29   The Move Toward the True Self

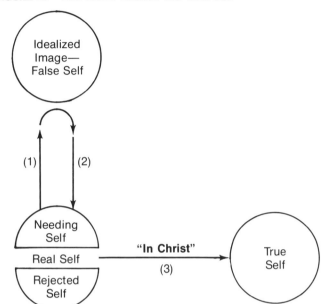

The Goal of Christian Therapy

The goal of Christian therapy is to work through the client's needing and rejected selves, and to reunite them into the true self. This is possible only through a self-acceptance (i.e., an acceptance of the real self) based on Christ's acceptance. As the needing and rejected selves give up their struggle to attain the idealized image, the client can experience wholeness and completeness in Christ.

What steps should the Christian counselor follow to assist the client to experience this wholeness? First, the counselor must ascertain the basic direction in which the troubled person is moving in order to cope with insecurities, anxiety, and depression. That is, is the client a "moving toward," "moving against," or "moving away" personality? Second, armed with this knowledge, the counselor will be able to determine the basic form of the client's idealized image. Third, to uncover the details of the image, the counselor needs to acquire and correlate a great deal of

specific data about the client: childhood fantasies, inherent abilities, needs, special personal experiences, individualized solutions to cope with internal conflicts, and so on. Fourth, the
counselor must deal with the client's idealized image, which, as
we have noted, is the source of major difficulties. For example,
it causes alienation from one's real self by introducing an impossible standard of perfection. Moreover, the individual becomes
"so alienated from his actual self by trying to live in his idealized
image that he can blame all his failures upon outside forces"
instead of himself (Bischof 1970, 21). The counselor must gradually show that the struggle to attain the idealized image is, as
Horney observed, a vain search for glory that can drain away
one's whole life:

> I now saw gradually that the neurotic's idealized image did not
> merely constitute a false belief in his value and significance; it
> was rather like the creation of a Frankenstein monster which in
> time usurped his best energies. It eventually usurped his drive to
> grow, to realize his given potentialities. And this meant that he
> was no longer interested in realistically tackling or outgrowing his
> difficulties, and in fulfilling his potentials, but was bent on ac-
> tualizing his idealized self. It entails not only the compulsive drive
> for worldly glory through success, power and triumph but also the
> tyrannical inner system by which he tries to mold himself into a
> godlike being; it entails neurotic claims and the development of
> neurotic pride [Horney 1950, 367–68]

Emergence of the true self, the ultimate goal of Christian counseling, can occur only as the individual faces and accepts the real
self. If the real self is in Christ, nothing about it should be avoided
or denied. In principle, Christians have no need for an idealized
image, the struggle to attain which betrays an inner rejection of
the real self. On the basis of Christ's death and unconditional
acceptance, Christians can face the real self without resorting to
Phariseeism and its futile flight from truth.

It was earlier explained that the three major types of personality are rooted in an inability to cope with the excessive needs
and rejection experienced by the real self. They are different
methods of trying to escape from the despised negative elements
of the real self. As the client comes to terms with and accepts

the real self, however, the extreme characteristics of the "moving toward," "moving against," and "moving away" personalities will accordingly diminish in intensity. No longer afraid to face the real self, the individual can gradually drop the unhealthy methods which were adopted to compensate for perceived shortcomings.

The goal of the Christian counselor, then, is to move as deeply as possible into the inner workings of the one being counseled. As we come to understand the counselee—the unique components of the needing and rejected self, the unique biological and environmental factors that have contributed to psychological makeup, and individualized solutions for dealing with insecurity (which include developing a particular type of personality and struggling to achieve the idealized image)—we will be able to determine which doctrines must be internalized if inner reconciliation is to take place. Paul's injunction, "Be reconciled to God" (2 Cor. 5:20), should stand as the Christian counselor's goal for every client. This reconciliation with God should be viewed as entailing both the eternal destiny and the inner emotional life of the counselee.

9

The Counsel of God*

We have several times alluded to the importance of incorporating appropriate Christian doctrines in the counseling process. Identifying the unique factors which have shaped a troubled individual's psychological makeup, knowing precisely where that person is, will help the counselor determine which theological points fit the particular situation. Through doctrinal self-disclosure the counselor can bring relevant Christian truths into the natural therapeutic flow. As the counselee is assisted to internalize and apply these doctrines, positive change occurs and personal identity is restored. Throughout the process it is vital for the counselor not only to know and recite these Christian teachings, but also to live them.

In this final chapter we will take a brief look at the counsel of God, those particular Christian teachings which have significant implications for the psychospiritual life. These teachings pertain to the process of salvation and the establishment of a new relationship with God.

We have observed that mental and emotional disorders are among the serious consequences of the fall. With the coming of salvation into the individual life, these consequences begin to be reversed. Redemption involves not only reconciliation with God, but healing of mental pathology as well. It is imperative to re-

*For the doctrinal explanations in this chapter I am indebted to Stephen Smallman.

189

member, however, that the consequences of the fall are so severe
that they are not immediately undone as soon as a right relationship with God is established. In his book *More than Redemption* Jay Adams suggests in effect that with salvation
emotional healing should come automatically. He does not seem
to take seriously enough the dire lasting impact of sin on the
human psyche. Consequently, his direct application of the experience of salvation to the process of mental or emotional healing is open to criticism as being somewhat superficial or
simplistic. We need to appreciate both the radical transformation
that comes to pass in our salvation and at the same time the fact
that the consequences which sin (in many instances the "sins of
the fathers") has had on the emotional life cannot be immediately
overcome.

At this point a basic distinction made by theologians will prove
very helpful for our study. On the one hand is the *accomplishment* of redemption, and on the other the *application* of redemption. The former concerns Christ's once-for-all purchase of
our redemption when He came to earth two thousand years ago.
The latter concerns our personal experience of salvation (what
the older theologians, such as Archibald Alexander, called "ex-
perimental religion"). The Westminster Shorter Catechism asks,
"How are we made partakers of the redemption purchased by
Christ?" and answers, "We are made partakers of the redemption
purchased by Christ, by the effectual application of it to us by
his Holy Spirit" (Question 29).

Just as the accomplishment of redemption by Christ can be
divided into a number of logical parts (incarnation, ministry, death,
resurrection, etc.), so the work of the Spirit in applying that redemption can be studied in terms of its parts as well as the whole.
A proper understanding of these components of the experience
of salvation will tell us much about the progress that can be
expected in emotional healing. Many people, misunderstanding
the theology of salvation, become unnecessarily discouraged at
what they view as lack of progress in holy living. It must be
remembered that salvation begins in the heart as we live our
earthly existence, but will be completed only when the believer
is glorified with Christ for eternity. The process of salvation,
then, is extensive, thorough, and continuing.

Figure 30 gives a visual presentation of the order in the application of salvation as that process is understood by most systematic theologians. The diagram reminds us that the essence of salvation is the person of Christ and our union with Him. The sections of the circle represent stages of our redemption "in Christ" (1 Cor. 1:30; Eph. 1:3–14). The idea of being "in Christ," including its implication for the fundamental matter of our identity, has been treated at some length in chapter 5. It is now possible to become more specific in terms of how the steps in our salvation experience carry over into psychological healing (as suggested by the terms outside the circle). What follows is a brief explanation of each step of salvation and then a more extensive

FIGURE 30 The Steps of Salvation and Their Implications for Psychological Healing

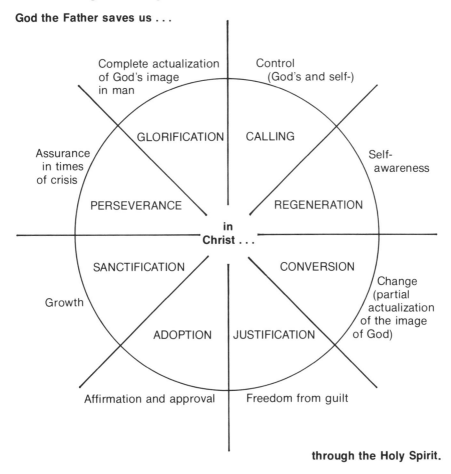

God the Father saves us . . .

through the Holy Spirit.

presentation of its implications for psychological healing. Fuller explanations of the doctrines themselves are readily available in most systematic theologies. (Particularly helpful inasmuch as it follows the order of this diagram is *Redemption: Accomplished and Applied* by John Murray.)

Calling

Calling is the work of God summoning us to faith in Jesus Christ. In that it is God who calls us, the call includes the power for us to respond. Thus the Westminster Catechism uses the term *effectual* calling: when God calls, *we come*. Probably the most vivid illustration of effectual calling is Jesus at the tomb of Lazarus. Jesus' "calling" to the dead man had effect. So also, when preaching Christ crucified to hostile Jews and Gentiles, Paul knew that although most would reject, "those whom God has called, both Jews and Greeks," would find Christ to be both "the power of God and the wisdom of God" (1 Cor. 1:22–25). Thus, calling refers to God's initiating the work of salvation in the hearts of those "dead in transgressions" (Eph. 2:4–5).

The doctrine of calling reminds us unequivocally that God is in control of His creation. He is personally and intimately involved in the lives of each of His children. Everything that relates to the child of God is in His loving control; this includes all external circumstances and situations, interpersonal relationships, the human body, brain chemistry, and the inner person (the heart). The believer can rest assured of, and respond to, God's control of every aspect of the enterprise of living.

We humans have the choice of submitting to God's control, or straining and pushing against it. In becoming a Christian one consciously acknowledges God's providential care and control. "God is in control of my life, and the more I cooperate with that control the more satisfied and contented I will be as God's child"— that is the way the Christian should reason. We find it hard, however, to give up trying to control our lives. We do not naturally submit to the control of others; on the contrary, we manipulate and maneuver in attempts to gain control over them. But Christians are to submit totally to God's control. To turn away from sinful impulses is a step toward eliminating destructive fighting against submission to God. That is one key to better mental health and spiritual functioning.

Submitting to God's control is often called "submitting to the will of God" or "doing the will of God." Both expressions indicate a need for Christians to so discipline their emotions and behavior as to give God full reign in their lives. The terms *self-control* and *ego strength* refer to a person's ability to control basic emotions and behavior. With the fall, of course, human beings lost control of the external (the world, history, the animal kingdom, and their own physical bodies, which are now subject to decay and death) and the internal (personal emotions, thought, and will). But when one becomes a Christian the Holy Spirit indwells the inner person and works to create a sound sense of self-control. "For God did not give us a spirit of timidity, but a spirit of power, of love and of self-discipline [ego strength]" (2 Tim. 1:7). And this self-discipline enables us to better submit to God's will. Thus, self-control and submitting to God's control are closely interrelated, for it is when we acknowledge God's control that the Holy Spirit works in us to develop our self-control, which issues in our submitting ourselves completely to God's will.

Regeneration

Regeneration is the actual change of heart brought about by the Holy Spirit. The classic discussion of regeneration is Jesus' conversation with Nicodemus in John 3. A careful reading of John 3 will show that Jesus is not commanding some action *from* Nicodemus. Rather Jesus is describing a work of the Spirit that must happen *to* Nicodemus or anyone else who would enter the kingdom of God. "You must be born again" is in the indicative, not the imperative; it is a declarative statement of what is absolutely necessary. Nicodemus could no more be the cause of his new birth than a nonexistent child can be the cause of his physical conception and birth. Accordingly, many translators suggest that "born again" might better be translated "begotten again" or even "begotten from above."

The act of regeneration occurs to some extent without our being conscious of it. This distinct, one-time work of the Holy Spirit brings conviction, preparing our heart to make a commitment to Christ. "When he [the Holy Spirit] comes, he will convict the world of guilt in regard to sin and righteousness and judgment" (John 16:8). In the act of regeneration the Holy Spirit makes us more self-aware. We become conscious of our sin, our lack of relationship with Christ, our need for righteousness in Christ, and the future judgment. We must become aware of these facts, so we can respond to Christ as Savior. Without such an awareness, we cannot feel or see any need of Christ, and consequently we will not respond to Christ's invitation.

The transformation begun at regeneration continues after conversion and throughout our life on earth. This process is usually called sanctification. After embracing Christ, Christians "walk in the Spirit," and the Spirit gradually brings to their consciousness particular areas of the heart that need to be changed and made more Christ-like. Openness to the truth about oneself, therefore, should be a continuing characteristic of Christian living. One's self-awareness should be even greater after conversion than before. Although new Christians are sometimes hesitant to be open to the truth about themselves, should we not be open to what God already knows and has accepted about us? For Christians to be more closed and repressed in this respect than they were before their conversion is inconsistent with the doctrine of regeneration and the essence of the Christian gospel.

The question is sometimes raised: "In light of our individual background, how responsible are we for our behavior?" The answer is that all Christians are responsible to be inwardly open to God's bringing to their consciousness those things about the self that need to be rectified and changed. A Christian need not fear to utter David's prayer, "Search me, O God" (Ps. 139:23), because God will not show us anything that He has not forgiven. To hide from ourselves is to deny God the chance to show us ways in which we His children can experience even closer relationship with Him.

Conversion

Conversion denotes the conscious choice to turn to Christ from a life of self-centeredness and sin. It involves repentance and faith. While conversion is made possible by the gracious work of God, it does not happen until man actually responds (Rom. 10:9–10, 13). In that conversions involve human response and are the visible or experiential witness to the invisible work of the Spirit, the various ways people experience conversion have been given a great deal of attention. Among some well-meaning evangelicals, conversion, and particularly crisis or sudden conversion, has been so emphasized that it is possible to come away with the idea that conversion is the only aspect of salvation worth mentioning. On the other hand, psychologists have often secularized conversion experiences, treating them simply as human phenomena. And indeed, what some people claim are conversions are nothing more than unusual psychological experiences. The assumption of this study is that while some "conversions" are not the genuine item, it is a fact of Scripture and of experience that there is a real spiritual conversion in which a person comes to know new life with God.

The doctrine of conversion assures us that we can change. Repentance and faith put us in a position for God to change our heart and perhaps even our basic personality structure. Such changes do not occur automatically, however. We often despair of changing inwardly. When we try to change old habits or ways of life, we fail over and over again. Yet we can be assured that, with conversion, personality change is possible. God has committed Himself to work in our lives both before and after conversion. "He who began a good work in you will carry it on to completion until the day of Christ Jesus" (Phil. 1:6). Change is not necessarily instantaneous, but it can always be expected.

The changes accompanying conversion occur within certain limits. Although the change is dynamic (from the old nature to the new nature, from the likeness of the first Adam to that of the second Adam, from darkness to light), God does not commit Himself to working instantaneous total change on the psychological level. Figure 13 (p. 89) will be helpful here. Becoming a Christian does not immediately return us or fully restore us to the image of God. Rather, we are placed on the road of renewal toward that image. The resulting psychological change may or may not be radical. In some personality types, especially those who have little sense of identity, the change may be much more telling than in those whose basic personality has always been quite stable.

Our repentance (a change of mind leading to a change of heart) calls for a change of lifestyle—turning from the world and turning to Christ. That change, however, must be initiated by God from within; only then does it properly become a matter of the human will. Change in lifestyle should reflect the change in personality God has wrought within the heart. After conversion many Christians make the mistake of trying to force themselves to live in a way that may not be congruent with their feelings. They need reminding that the most significant change is not behavioral so much as attitudinal. It is a matter of the heart, not of outward actions. Conversion is fundamentally a radical reorientation of identity (as we defined it earlier), that is, of who one is. The Christian has a new heart, mind, and status with God; that is the significant change.

The dynamics of conversion are such that before the actual event one often goes through a long period of unrest and upheaval. That is followed by the embracing of an ideal, a new life philosophy. Afterwards there is a stage of relief and peace, which is followed by propagation of the ideal or philosophy to others (see Figure 31). The amount of discomfort before actual conversion will probably determine the quantity of behavioral change, though not necessarily the quality. Although change is an integral part of being converted, we must guard against expecting too much change of ourselves at the moment of new life—or demanding too much afterwards. In all of this it is to be remembered that the most vital consideration is the individual's new identity, not the period of propagation. That will naturally follow if one has truly become a Christian.

FIGURE 31   The Dynamics of Conversion

Justification

The Bible ties two momentous transactions to the exercise of faith—justification and adoption (Rom. 3:21–24; 8:12–16; Gal. 2:16–20; 3:26–4:7). Both of these transactions are single events rather than processes. In justification we are declared righteous because of the righteousness of Christ, whose death atoned for our sin. Since we are now seen as righteous, God also declares us to be adopted into the family of God, whose oldest and only "natural" Son is none other than Jesus Himself. Neither justification nor atonement requires worthiness on the part of the recipient; they are gifts of God based on the worthiness of Christ. The discovery of this great truth has actually brought about conversions. Probably the most prominent of these was that of Martin Luther, who felt himself to be born again when he discovered through a study of the Book of Romans that we can be made just, or righteous, before God simply by believing that Christ is our righteousness. Justification and adoption are companion doctrines, but their implications for emotional healing need to be explained separately.

The doctrine of justification has significant implications for handling and removing feelings of guilt. Guilt can cripple emotional health by causing depression and eroding self-esteem. The Christian community has tended to distinguish between true guilt and false guilt, the latter referring to the sense of guilt which arises as a result of the judgments and disapproval of men. False guilt occurs when we violate social taboos, suffer feelings of inferiority, or find that for some reason we are not accepted by others or even perhaps by ourselves (Tournier 1962, 65–66). True guilt, on the other hand, concerns our standing before God; it is felt when we are disobedient to Him or unwilling to place our faith in Him. "This is not something that results from criticisms of men. It comes when people in their innermost hearts experience reproach and judgment from God" (Collins 1973, 185). While the humanistic or "self" movements in psychology have little remedy for any guilt feelings, this is especially the case with true guilt.

Bruce Narramore and Bill Counts distinguish between psychological and theological guilt. Psychological guilt is the internalization of the experience of being rejected or shamed by one's parents (or some other significant person in one's life); it involves self-rejection ("I'm not worthy") or self-shame ("I always blow it") (Narramore and Counts 1974, 34). Narramore and Counts point out that nowhere in the New Testament is psychological guilt regarded as a desirable or constructive feeling. In fact, Paul says that worldly sorrow leads to death, but godly sorrow (i.e., theological guilt) can lead to life (2 Cor. 7:10). Theological guilt is the objective breaking of God's laws as they are recorded in the Bible, with the consequent feeling of having failed in one's relationship with God. If we respond to theological guilt in the proper way, it can lead to reconciliation and restoration of a full relationship with God.

In chapter 8 we discussed the "moving toward," "moving against," and "moving away" personalities. Each type of personality, of course, experiences feelings of guilt, and, as might be expected, handles them in its own unique way (see Figure 32). In the "moving toward" personality, guilt feelings are likely to be accompanied by the belief that God is angry—"God is so angry with me that He may permanently reject me; therefore, I must do all I can to please Him and get back in His good graces." Every time guilt is felt, it is projected into the conviction that God is angry and rejecting. This creates fear or perhaps even panic. The basic solution is to try to work one's way back into God's favor. Christians with "moving toward" personalities aim at a life which they think will appease God's anger and insure His acceptance and affirmation. There are two basic flaws here. First, the position ascribed to God (anger at and permanent rejection of the individual) is doubtless not His position at all. Second, it is a grave error to think that one can earn God's acceptance by works.

The "moving against" personality is generally not greatly disturbed by guilt feelings, and at times may even seem incapable of feeling true guilt or remorse. Such guilt as is felt will tend to set the "moving against" personality in opposition to God and create a rebellious "I don't care" attitude which manifests itself in continuation of whatever activity prompted the sense of guilt. These guilt feelings, then, will not result in true repentance, although many "moving against" personality types can fake repentance very convincingly, often misleading others by their apparent sincerity. But like Saul of the Old Testament, they lack real faith and the spirit of repentance.

"Moving away" personalities are likely to make every conceivable attempt to keep at a distance from God. Feeling guilty shakes their sense of self-sufficiency and unassailability. Therefore, the "moving away" individual will try to avoid guilt at all costs so as not to feel vulnerable. If real guilt is experienced, an attitude of "I don't care" or "I'll do better" may result. This

FIGURE 32 Improper Responses to Guilt Feelings

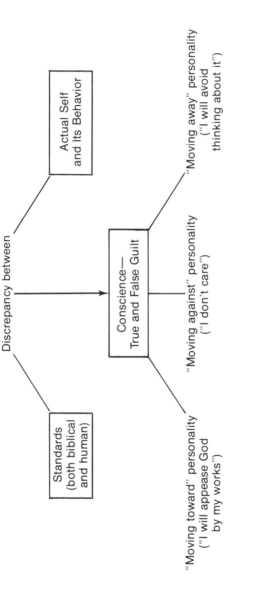

should not be confused with the rebellion of the "moving against" personality. It is actually an emotional detachment from the problem, an avoidance of any kind of deep relationship with God. Guilt, then, will drive the "moving away" individual even farther from Him. Christians who tend toward this type of personality need to be reminded that God does not desert His children, but like the father of the prodigal son wishes to meet men and women where they are when they feel guilty and alienated.

It is obvious that none of the three personality types makes a proper response to guilt. What, then, is the proper response? Awareness of guilt should lead us to repent swiftly and concisely, and to reconcile ourselves with Christ. Restoration to a full relationship with God will follow (see Figure 33). Guilt feelings can then be forgotten (Narramore and Counts 1974, 357). Note that this applies to both true and false guilt, which are often difficult to distinguish and both of which require restoration.

FIGURE 33   Proper Response to Guilt

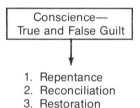

First, someone who experiences guilt feelings must repent, that is, be sorry for the behavior that has caused the guilt and make every effort to turn from it in order to renew relationship with Christ. Reconciliation with Christ should follow, since He has already taken the guilt and sin on Himself in the atonement. One must never fail to reconcile with Christ. If repentant individuals fail to do so, it is probably because they feel that, to be accepted, they have to live up to a personal idealized image (which they imagine Christ has set for them).

The process of reconciliation can occur only if we have compassion for ourselves. As Christ demonstrated compassion for us, so too, on the basis of Christ's acceptance of us, we must be compassionate with ourselves. In His compassion Christ has taken all the punishment, rejection, and shame that any person could ever experience. Since on the cross Christ bore all these burdens for us, it is only reasonable that as Christians we should not allow them to erode our feelings of self-esteem or to cause us neurotic depressions. The proper response to guilt, then, is repentance, reconciliation, and restoration to relationship with God. Although we will continue to experience a measure of guilt throughout our earthly lives, it must not be allowed to lead to self-hatred or other destructive emotions. Rather, what has been accomplished by God's grace must ever be kept in mind:

> From the limited viewpoint of our internal self-perception, we may continue to feel guilty before our own negated values and God's; but our condition before God, from the point of view of the ground and giver of values, has changed. We exist in an undiminished covenant with the unconditional valuer. How one temporarily feels about oneself is different from who one is before God. The truly penitent are forgiven, despite the tenacity of all recurring guilt feelings to deny that amazing grace.
>
> So how does guilt-free Christianity differ from its secular counterparts? It frees us from demonic self-destructive guilt through atonement: God's Son died for our sins. We are freed from guilt-laden idolatry by being shown that the One who gives both creaturehood and finitude, and finally the One who takes it all away in death, has made Himself known as trustworthy. If I am unconditionally valued amid my value negations, I am freed from the harried need to hear the neighbor's claim. The self-deceptive rigidities under which guilt has carried on its clandestine operations are themselves disarmed by this freeing Word. [Oden 1980, 117]

Adoption

Our adoption, God's acceptance of us as His children, has deep implications, and especially for those who never received any notable affirmative input from their parents. Many people have been raised in less than ideal backgrounds. Once they come to realize that God is their parent, they will experience a sense of approval such as they have never had before. The step of regarding God as one's parent is voluntary, open to every child of God. At age twelve Jesus asked His parents when they found Him lingering in the temple, "Didn't you know I had to be in my Father's house?" His mother had asked, "Son, why have you treated us like this? Your father and I have been anxiously searching for you" (Luke 2:48–49). It must have come as a shock to Joseph to hear Jesus refer to God as His Father. Yet we too must acknowledge that we have both human parents and a heavenly parent. It has been pointed out that our earthly parents must come to be regarded as "emeritus" or secondary parents, giving way to the heavenly Father as our primary parent. Through heavenly adoption Christians are given a new relationship in which they come to know God intimately and lovingly as their Father. The positive emotional consequences of this affirming relationship will be significant and lasting.

Sanctification

Sanctification is the spiritual equivalent of the growth of a newly born child (see the discussion of "Regeneration," pp. 193–94). Unlike justification and adoption, which are granted immediately to the believer, sanctification is a gradual process that takes place within the believer. In justification one is declared righteous once and for all because of the sacrifice of Christ. In sanctification one is continuously being made righteous, that is, more and more Christ-like, through the working of the Holy Spirit. While some claim that complete sanctification is possible in this life, most Christian thinkers understand the Bible to teach that the work of sanctification entails constant struggles and growth, and will continue throughout this earthly life.

Sanctification insures the Christian's continued psychospiritual growth toward maturity. God's goal is for each Christian to develop as fully as possible his or her own unique talents, abilities, and gifts. Unfortunately, Christian growth is often stifled from within, by selfishness or fear, or from without, by churches that tend to make new Christians fit into preconceived molds. The body of Christ must allow all its members to grow in accord with the plan which God has for each of them.

Fear keeps us from growing. We would rather rest in the security of what we are now than stride off to take unknown risks.

> Every human being has both sets of forces within him. One set clings to safety and defensiveness out of fear, tending to regress backward, hanging on to the past, afraid to grow away from the

primitive communication with the mother's uterus and breast, afraid to take chances, afraid to jeopardize what he already has, afraid of independence, freedom and separateness. The other set of forces impels him forward toward wholeness of self, toward full functioning of all his capacities, toward confidence in the face of the external world at the same time that he can accept his deepest, real, unconscious self. . . .

Safety ◄──────── 〈 Person 〉 ────────► Growth

. . . Safety has both anxieties and delights, growth has both anxieties and delights. We grow forward when the delights of growth and anxieties of safety are greater than the anxieties of growth and the delights of safety. [Maslow 1968, 46–47]

There is indeed a natural tendency in all of us to fear growth, to cling to personality features that hold us back, even to regress. This is understandable, for growth always entails risk. Yet Christians ought to seize the opportunity to grow, for God will work with them and the Holy Spirit will be their teacher. That God has adopted us as His children and will watch over us frees us from the desire and need to cling to safety and allows us to grow toward Christ. As far as the possibilities for our growth are concerned, the Christian faith, unlike the "human potential" movement, knows no limit, for the growth of the Christian is a matter of God's ongoing work of sanctification.

Regardless of how clearly we believe we understand the process of growth, growth is God's business. Rather than our pushing him, he is calling us, beckoning us to follow, as he seeks to overcome our reluctance to trust him. The very nature of growth prevents our controlling it. One does not crucify himself, he is crucified. Nor can one resurrect himself. Dying means dying to everything that would demand anything of ourselves so that we receive again what God has to give. In responding to his overture with faith we are restored to the domain of hope. Because God is pushing us— to give us all that we need for our fulfillment—we can trust him in each present moment. He is present to change it from despair to hope, from reversal to victory, from illusion to reality, from monotony to joy.

Without this trust, we fear to break new ground. As creatures of habit we tend to repeat the past and hold on to our illusions. We find our security in what is familiar. The new is alienating until we have reason to trust. In a day of social change such as ours many are trying desperately to rediscover the old. Actually they are looking in the wrong direction for their security. Since a day of change shakes us loose from our traditional ways of doing things, we are actually freed up to enter the new. But whether we will or not depends on whom if anyone we trust. . . . Trust itself is meaningful. . . . Nietzsche . . . said, "He who has a why to live for can bear with almost any how." For the Christian the why is not as important as the Who. Trust centers in a person. He who knows the Who and trusts him, can bear with almost any how or what, even though he does not know the why. In fact, he may feel little need to search for the why. . . . Growth is a process based on a state of being—a state of being loved—a state of grace. [Hulme 1978, 54–55]

Perseverance

Scripture teaches godly perseverance. This has a twofold meaning. On the one hand, Scripture teaches that God will persevere with those whom He is in the process of saving (Rom. 8:28–39, particularly v. 30, which states that those whom God has called and justified are the ones who will be glorified). On the other hand, Scripture urges those whom God saves to demonstrate their salvation by persevering in the face of all difficulties (2 Peter 1:3–11). Thus *we* persevere—but we are able to do so because we are on the rock that can never be moved. The "perseverance of the saints" should more properly be called the "perseverance of God."

Christians can be assured that in times of crisis and conflict God will be near. No crisis or conflict has the power to overwhelm us. We can rest in the assurance that our Father is in control of the circumstances of our life. He will supply all the resources necessary to cope with whatever difficulties arise. "No temptation has seized you except what is common to man. And God is faithful; he will not let you be tempted beyond what you can bear. But when you are tempted, he will also provide a way out so that you can stand up under it" (1 Cor. 10:13).

Paul sounded the note that he had learned to be content in all circumstances because he was in Christ and found strength there. For our days on earth God has promised, "Never will I leave you;

never will I forsake you" (Heb. 13:5). God's presence with us now in the Holy Spirit is a foretaste of a life of glory in heaven. The doctrine of perseverance is God's promise that His gracious hand always supports us.

Glorification

Glorification is that future act of God by which we will finally become what He has saved us to be, His sons and daughters who perfectly reflect the "firstborn among many brothers" (Rom. 8:29). We presently possess this potential by virtue of our union with Christ, who is already glorified. Romans 8:30 tells us that "those he justified, he also glorified." The verbs are in the past tense, signifying that the action referred to has already been accomplished. We will not actually experience glorification, however, until the day of resurrection and the return of Christ (1 Cor. 15:50–57).

At the moment of glorification the image of God will be fully actualized in the believer. What was partially accomplished in conversion will be completed in glorification. The results of this process are beyond our imagination, yet we know that we will be completely in the image of God and will live in the home for which we have hoped—"a new heaven and a new earth, the home of righteousness." The moment we first see the face of Jesus we will be made into His image.

> Dear friends, now we are children of God, and what we will be has not yet been made known. But we know that when he appears, we shall be like him, for we shall see him as he is. [1 John 3:2]

> And we, who with unveiled faces all reflect the Lord's glory, are being transformed into his likeness with ever-increasing glory, which comes from the Lord, who is the Spirit. [2 Cor. 3:18]

While Christians eagerly anticipate their glorification, it should be noted that this event will not occur at the time of physical death, when believers pass into the presence of the Lord. Failure to understand this has sometimes caused young believers to suffer from false guilt. They conclude that because they are not eager to die, they are not good Christians. They erroneously reason that good Christians ought to be excited about the prospect of dying since that will be their day of glory. Actually that day will come in God's time, not at the moment of death.

The doctrines which we have briefly examined in this chapter describe, in essence, God's gradual transformation of the "being" dimension of the human personality. The eight steps in the redemptive process are God's work in our hearts as He makes us into the persons we were originally designed to be—whole beings who worship their Creator. Figure 34 illustrates that all aspects of the Christian life center on the "being" dimension of personality, not the "doing" dimension. All pastoral work, then, including Christian counseling, must focus on the heart.

FIGURE 34   Being—The Center of the Christian Life

God has called us to a life of intimate relationship with Him. Psychological healing is to be found in that relationship and in the restoration of the identity which God gave to the human race at the time of creation. Christian counselors can help heal the emotional problems of their clients by reviewing with them the steps of salvation, concentrating on those doctrines relevant to the particular situation, and integrating those doctrines with psychological theory. That kind of counseling, carrying the work of God into the counselee's heart, will have positive and lasting consequences, for as Christian counselors we can rely on this promise from God:

I took you from the ends of the earth, from its farthest corners I called you. I said, "You are my servant"; I have chosen you and have not rejected you. So do not fear, for I am with you; do not be dismayed, for I am your God. I will strengthen you and help you; I will uphold you with my righteous right hand. [Isa. 41:9–10]

Preface to *A Discourse on Trouble of Mind and the Disease of Melancholy*
Timothy Rogers (1658–1728)

1. Look upon your distressed friends as under one of the worst distempers to which this miserable life is exposed. Melancholy incapacitates them for thought or action: it confounds and disturbs all their thoughts and fills them with vexation and anguish. I verily believe, that when this malign state of mind is deeply fixed and has spread its deleterious influence over every part, it is as vain to attempt to resist it by reasoning and rational motives, as to oppose a fever or the gout or pleurisy. One of the very worst attendants of this disease is the want of sleep, by which in other distresses men are relieved and refreshed; but in this disease, either sleep flies far away, or is so disturbed that the poor sufferer, instead of being refreshed, is like one on the rack. The faculties of the soul are weakened, and all their operations disturbed and clouded: and the poor body languishes and pines away at the same time. And that which renders this disease more formidable is its long continuance. It is a long time often before it comes to its height; and it is usually as tedious in its declension. It is in every respect sad and overwhelming, a state of darkness that has no discernible beams of light. It generally begins in the body and

then conveys its venom to the mind. I pretend not to tell you what medicines will cure it, for I know of none. I leave you to advise with such as are skilled in physic, and especially to such doctors as have experienced something of it themselves; for it is impossible to understand the nature of it in any other way than by experience. There is danger, as Richard Greenham says, "that the bodily physician will look no further than the body, while the spiritual physician will totally disregard the body, and look only at the mind.

2. Treat those who are under this disease with tender compassion. Remember also that you are liable to the same affliction; for however brisk your spirits and lively your feelings now, you may meet with such reverses, with such long and sharp afflictions, as will sink your spirits. Many, not naturally inclined to melancholy, have, by overwhelming and repeated calamities, been sunk into this dark gulf.

3. Never use harsh language to your friends when under the disease of melancholy. This will only serve to fret and perplex them the more, but will never benefit them. I know that the counsel of some is to rebuke and chide them on all occasions; but I dare confidently say that such advisors never felt the disease themselves; for if they had, they would know that thus they do pour oil into the flames, and chafe and exasperate their wounds, instead of healing them. John Dod, by reason of his mild, meek, merciful spirit, was reckoned one of the fittest persons to deal with those thus afflicted. Never was any person more tender and compassionate, as all will be convinced, who will read the accounts of Mr. Peacock and Mrs. Drake, both of whom were greatly relieved by his conversation.

4. If you would possess any influence over your friends in this unhappy state of mind, you must be careful not to express any want of confidence in what they relate of their own feelings and distresses. On this point there is often a great mistake. When they speak of their frightful and distressing apprehensions, it is common for friends to reply "that this is all imaginary." . . . [But their fear] is a real one, and their misery is as real as any experienced by man. It is true, their imagination is disordered, but this is merely the effect of a deeper disease. These afflicted persons never can believe that you have any real sympathy with their misery or . . . feel any compassion for them, unless you believe what they say.

5. Do not urge your melancholy friends to do what is out of their power. They are like persons whose bones are broken, and who are incapacitated for action. Their disease is accompanied with perplexing and tormenting thought; if you can innocently divert them, you would do them a great kindness; but do not urge them to do anything which requires close and intent thinking; this will only increase the disease. But you will ask, ought we not to urge them to hear the Word of God? I answer, if they are so far gone in the disease as to be in continual, unremitting anguish, they are not capable of hearing, on account of the painful disorder of their minds. But if their disorder is not come to such a distressing height, you may kindly and gently persuade them to attend on preaching of the Word; but beware of using a peremptory and violent method. The method pursued by John Dod with Mrs. Drake should be imitated. "The burden which overloaded her soul was so great, that we never durst add any thereunto, but fed her with all encouragements, she being too apt to overcharge herself, and to despair upon any addition of fuel to that fire which was inwardly consuming her." And so, wherever she went to hear, notice was given to the minister officiating, that he had such a hearer, and by this means she received no discouragement from hearing.

6. Do not attribute the effects of mere disease to the devil; although I do not deny that he has any agency in producing some disease; especially, by harassing and disturbing the mind to such a degree, that the body suffers with it. But it is very unwise to ascribe every feeling and every word of the melancholy man to Satan; whereas, many of these are as natural consequences of bodily disease, as the symptoms of a fever, which the poor sufferer can no more avoid, than the sick man can keep himself from sighing and groaning. Many will say to such a one, "Why do you so pore over your case and thus gratify the devil?" whereas it is the very nature of the disease to cause such fixed musings. You might as well say to a man in a fever, "Why are you not well, why will you be sick?" Some indeed suppose that the melancholy hug their disease, and are unwilling to give it up, but you might as well suppose that a man would be pleased with lying on a bed of thorns, or in a fiery furnace. No doubt the devil knows how to work on minds thus diseased, and by shooting his fiery darts he endeavors to drive them to utter despair. But if you persuade them that all which they experience is from the devil,

you may induce the opinion in them that they are actually possessed of the evil one; which has been the unhappy condition of some whose minds were disordered. I would not have you to bring a railing accusation even against the devil, neither must you falsely accuse your friends by saying that they gratify him.

7. Do not express much surprise or wonder at anything which melancholy persons say or do. What will not they say, who are in despair of God's mercy? What will not they do, who think themselves lost forever? You know that even such a man as Job cursed his day, so that the Lord charged him with "darkening counsel by words without knowledge." Do not wonder that they give expression to bitter complaints; the tongue will always be speaking of the aching tooth. Their soul is sore vexed, and although they get no good by complaining, yet they cannot but complain, to find themselves in such a doleful case. And they say with David, "I am weary with my groaning: all the night make I my bed to swim. I water my couch with my tears"; yet they cannot forbear to groan and weep more, until their very eyes be consumed with grief. Let no sharp words of theirs provoke you to talk sharply to them. Sick people are apt to be peevish, and it would be a great weakness in you not to bear with them, when you see that a long and sore disease has deprived them of their former good temper.

8. Do not tell them any frightful stories, nor recount to them the sad disasters which have overtaken others. Their hearts already meditate terror, and by every alarming thing of which they hear they are the more terrified, and their disordered imagination is prepared to seize upon every frightful image which is presented. The hearing of sad things always causes them more violent agitations. Yet you must avoid merriment and levity in their presence, for this would lead them to think that you have no sympathy with them, nor concern for them. A mixture of gravity and affableness will best suit them; and if I might advise, I would counsel parents not to put their children, who are naturally inclined to melancholy, to learning, or to any employment which requires much study; lest they should at length be preyed upon by their own thoughts.

9. Do not, however, think it needless to talk with them. But do not speak as if you thought their disease would be of long continuance; for this is the prospect which appears most gloomy

to the melancholy. Rather encourage them to hope for speedy deliverance. Endeavor to revive their spirits by declaring that God can give them relief in a moment, and that He has often done so with others; that He can quickly heal their disease, and cause His amiable and reconciled face to shine upon them.

10. It will be useful to tell them of others who have been in the same state of suffering and yet have been delivered. It is indeed true that they who are depressed by such a load of grief are with difficulty persuaded that any were ever in such a condition as they are. They think themselves to be more wicked than Cain or Judas, and view their own cases to be entirely singular. It will, therefore, be important to relate real cases of deliverance from similar distress and darkness. Several such cases have been known to me, as that of Mr. Rosewell, and also Mr. Porter, both ministers of the gospel. The latter was six years under the pressure of melancholy; yet both these experienced complete deliverance, and afterwards rejoiced in the light of God's countenance. I myself was near two years in great pain of body, and greater pain of soul, and without any prospect of peace or help and yet God recovered me by His sovereign grace and mercy. Robert Bruce, minister in Edinburgh, was twenty years in terrors of conscience, and yet delivered afterwards. And so many others, who after dark and stormy night were blessed with the cheerful light of returning day. John Foxe, in his "Book of Martyrs," gives an account of a certain John Glover, who was worn and consumed with inward trouble for five years, so that he had no comfort in his food, nor in his sleep, nor in any enjoyment in life. He was so perplexed, as if he had been in the deepest pit of hell, and yet this good servant of God, after all these horrid temptations and buffetings of Satan, was delivered from all his trouble, and the effect was such a degree of mortification of sin, that he appeared as one already in heaven.

11. The next thing which you are to do for your melancholy friends is to pray for them. As they have not light and composure to pray for themselves, let your eyes weep for them in secret, and there let your souls melt in fervent holy prayers. You know that none but God alone can help them. Mr. Peacock said to John Dod, and his other friends, "Take not the name of God in vain, by praying for such a reprobate." Mr. Dod replied, "If God stir up your friends to pray for you, He will stir up Himself to hear their

prayers." You ought to consider that nothing but prayer can do them good. It is an obstinate disease that nothing else will overcome. Those who can cure themselves by resorting to wine and company, were never under this disease.

12. Nor only pray for them yourself, but engage other Christian friends also to pray for them. When many good people join their requests together, their cry is more acceptable and prevalent. When the church united in prayer for Peter in chains, he was soon delivered, and in the very time of their prayers. All believers have, through Christ, a great interest in heaven, and the Father is willing to grant what they unitedly and importunately ask in the name of His dear Son. I myself have been greatly helped by the prayers of others, and I heartily thank all those especially who set apart particular days to remember at a throne of grace my distressed condition. Blessed be God that He did not turn away His mercy from me, nor turn a deaf ear to their supplications!

13. Put your poor afflicted friends in mind, continually, of the sovereign grace of God in Jesus Christ. Often impress on their minds that He is merciful and gracious; that as far as the heavens are above the earth, so far are His thoughts above their thoughts; His thoughts of mercy above their self-condemning, guilty thoughts. Teach them, as much as you can, to look unto God, by the great mediator, for grace and strength, and not too much to pore over their own souls, where there is so much darkness and unbelief. And turn away their thoughts from the decrees of God. Show them what great sinners God has pardoned, and encourage them to believe and to hope for mercy. When Mrs. Drake was in her deplorable state of darkness, she would send a description of her case to distinguished ministers, concealing her name, to know whether such a creature, without natural affection, who had resisted and abused all means, could have any hope of going to heaven. Their answer was, that such like, and much worse, might by the mercy of God be received into favor, converted and saved; which did much allay her trouble. "For," said she, "the fountain of all my misery hath been that I sought that in the law which I should have found in the Gospel; and for that in myself, which was only to be found in Christ." From my own experience, I can testify that the mild and gentle way of dealing with such is the best.

Bibliography

Adams, J. E. 1970. *Competent to counsel.* Philadelphia: Presbyterian and Reformed.

———. 1973. *The Christian counselor's manual.* Grand Rapids: Baker.

———. 1975. *The use of the Scriptures in counseling.* Philadelphia: Presbyterian and Reformed.

———. 1977. *What about nouthetic counseling?* Grand Rapids: Baker.

———. 1980. *More than redemption.* Grand Rapids: Baker.

Alexander, A. 1978 reprint. *Thoughts on religious experience.* Edinburgh: Banner of Truth Trust.

Andersen, F. I. 1976. *Job,* ed. D. J. Wiseman. Tyndale Old Testament Commentary Series. Downers Grove, Ill.: Inter-Varsity.

Applewhite, B. 1980. *Feeling good about your feelings.* Wheaton, Ill.: Victor.

Ard, B. N., Jr., ed. 1966. *Counseling and psychotherapy.* Palo Alto: Science and Behavior Books.

Bailey, K. 1973. *The cross and the prodigal.* St. Louis: Concordia.

Bainton, R. 1950. *Here I stand.* New York: New American Library.

———, ed. 1963. *Studies on the Reformation.* Boston: Beacon.

Barbara, D. A. 1958. *Your speech reveals your personality.* Springfield, Ill.: Charles C. Thomas.

Barclay, W. 1974. *New Testament words.* Philadelphia: Westminster.

Bavinck, H. 1956. *Our reasonable faith,* trans. Henry Zylstra. Grand Rapids: Eerdmans.

Behm, J. 1965. Kapdia in the New Testament. In *Theological dictionary of the New Testament,* ed. G. Kittel and trans. G. W. Bromiley. Vol. 3. Grand Rapids: Eerdmans.

Berenson, B. G., and K. M. Mitchell. 1974. *Confrontation: For better or for worse.* Amherst, Mass.: Human Resource Development.

Berkhof, L. 1963. *Systematic theology.* London: Banner of Truth Trust.

Bischof, L. J. 1970. *Interpreting personality theories.* New York: Harper and Row.

Bobgan, M. and D. 1979. *The psychological way—the spiritual way.* Minneapolis: Bethany Fellowship.

Branden, N. 1976. In *Self-esteem,* ed. C. Ellison. Oklahoma City: Southwestern.

Brandon, O. R. 1966. Heart. In *Baker's dictionary of theology,* ed. E. F. Harrison. Grand Rapids: Baker.

Burns, R. B. 1980. *Psychology for the health professions.* Lancaster, England: MTP.

Burtt, E. A. 1954. *Metaphysical foundations of modern science.* Garden City, N.Y.: Doubleday.

Carey, G. 1977. *I believe in man.* Grand Rapids: Eerdmans.

Carkhuff, R. R., and B. G. Berenson. 1977. *Beyond counseling and therapy.* 2nd ed. New York: Holt, Rinehart & Winston.

Carter, J. D. 1975. Adams' theory of nouthetic counseling. *Journal of Psychology and Theology* 3:146–52.

————. 1977. Secular and sacred models of psychology and religion. *Journal of Psychology and Theology* 5:197–208.

Chambers, O. 1931. *Baffled to fight better.* London: Marshall, Morgan and Scott.

Chapman, A. H. 1976. *Harry Stack Sullivan: His life and his work.* New York: Putnam.

Colby, K. M. 1951. *A primer for psychotherapists.* New York: Ronald.

Collins, G. R. 1973. *The Christian psychology of Paul Tournier.* Grand Rapids: Baker.

Darling, H. W. 1969. *Man in triumph.* Grand Rapids: Zondervan.

Day, R. E. 1955. *The shadow of the broad brim.* Valley Forge, Pa.: Judson.

Delitzsch, F. 1977 reprint. *A system of biblical psychology.* Grand Rapids: Baker.

DiCaprio, N. S. 1974. *Personality theories: Guides to living.* Philadelphia: Saunders.

Douglas, J. D., ed. 1962. *New Bible dictionary.* Grand Rapids: Eerdmans.

Dye, D. L. 1966. *Faith and the physical world.* Grand Rapids: Eerdmans.

Egan, G. 1975. *The skilled helper.* Monterey, Calif.: Brooks/Cole.

————. 1977. *Interpersonal living: A skills/contract approach to human relations training in groups.* Monterey, Calif.: Brooks/Cole.

Faber, H., and E. van der Schoot. 1962. *The art of pastoral conversation.* Nashville: Abingdon.

Felker, D. W. 1974. *Building positive self-concepts.* Minneapolis: Burgess.

Fenichel, O. 1945. *The psychoanalytic theory of neurosis.* New York: Norton.

Gaylin, W. 1976. *Caring.* New York: Knopf.

Gazda, G. M. 1973. *Human relations development.* Boston: Allyn and Bacon.

Gergen, K. J. 1971. *The concept of self.* New York: Holt, Rinehart & Winston.

Glasser, W. 1972. *The identity society.* New York: Harper and Row.

Goble, F. G. 1970. *The third force.* New York: Grossman.

Gordon, T. 1975. *Teacher effectiveness training.* New York: Peter H. Wyden.

Gruber, M. 1980. Was Cain angry or depressed? Background of a biblical murder. *Biblical Archaeology Review,* December 1980, 35–36.

Guntrip, H. 1971. *Psychoanalytic theory, therapy, and the self.* New York: Basic Books.

Hammond, D. C., et al. 1977. *Improving therapeutic communication.* San Francisco: Jossey-Bass.

Hodge, M. B. 1967. *Your fear of love.* Garden City, N.Y.: Doubleday.

Hoffman, J. C. 1979. *Ethical confrontation in counseling.* Chicago: University of Chicago.

Hood, J. 1979. *Confrontation: A psychological and biblical perspective.* Unpublished master's thesis. Trinity Evangelical Divinity School.

Horney, K. 1937. *Neurotic personality of our times.* New York: Norton.

————. 1939. *New ways in psychoanalysis.* New York: Norton.

————. 1942. *Self-analysis.* New York: Norton.

————. 1945. *Our inner conflicts.* New York: Norton.

————. 1950. *Neurosis and human growth.* New York: Norton.

Howard, J. G. 1979. *The trauma of transparency.* Portland, Ore.: Multnomah.

Howe, R. L. 1953. *Man's need and God's action.* New York: Seabury.

Hulme, W. E. 1968. *Dialogue in despair.* Nashville: Abingdon.

————. 1970. *Pastoral care come of age.* Nashville: Abingdon.

————. 1978. *Your potential under God.* Minneapolis: Augsburg.

Jastrow, R. 1978. *God and the astronomers.* New York: Norton.

Johnson, W. E. 1980. Depression: Biochemical abnormality or spiritual backsliding? *Journal of the American Scientific Association,* March 1980, 18–27.

Laing, R. 1965. *The divided self.* Baltimore: Penguin.

Lake, D. M. 1975. Mind. In *Zondervan pictorial encyclopedia of the Bible,* ed. M. C. Tenney. Vol. 4. Grand Rapids: Zondervan.

Lewis, J. M. 1978. *To be a therapist.* New York: Brunner/Mazel.

Lewis, P. 1975. *The genius of Puritanism.* Sussex: Cary.

Maslow, A. H. 1954. *Motivation and personality.* New York: Harper and Row.

————. 1968. *Toward a psychology of being.* New York: Van Nostrand.

Mavis, W. C. 1963. *The psychology of Christian experience.* Grand Rapids: Zondervan.

Mayeroff, M. 1971. *On caring.* New York: Harper and Row.

Murray, J. 1955. *Redemption: Accomplished and applied.* Grand Rapids: Eerdmans.

Narramore, B., and B. Counts. 1974. *Freedom from guilt.* Irvine, Calif.: Harvest House.

Oden, T. C. 1978. *Kerygma and counseling.* New York: Harper and Row.

————. 1980. *Guilt free.* Nashville: Abingdon.

Oglesby, W. B., Jr. 1980. *Biblical themes for pastoral care.* Nashville: Abingdon.

Packer, J. I. 1973. *Knowing God.* Downers Grove, Ill.: Inter-Varsity.

————. 1978. *Knowing man.* Westchester, Ill.: Good News.

Patterson, C. H. 1974. *Relationship counseling and psychotherapy.* New York: Harper and Row.

Polanyi, M. 1964. *Personal knowledge.* New York: Harper and Row.

Rubins, J. L. 1972. In *Interpreting personality,* ed. A. M. Freedman and H. I. Kaplan. New York: Atheneum.

Sanders, J. A. 1972. *Torah and canon.* Philadelphia: Fortress.

Sanderson, J. W. 1972. *Epistemology.* Chattanooga: Signal.

Schaeffer, F. A. 1968. *The God who is there.* Downers Grove, Ill.: Inter-Varsity.

————. 1969. *Death in the city.* Chicago: Inter-Varsity.

————. 1971. *True spirituality.* Wheaton, Ill.: Tyndale.

Skoglund, E. 1979. The gold of depression. *Eternity,* June 1979, 50–52.

Smith, R. D. 1977. A physician looks at counseling: Depression. *Journal of Pastoral Practice* 1:85–87.

Sproul, R. C. 1974. *The psychology of atheism.* Minneapolis: Bethany Fellowship.

Spurgeon, C. H. 1880. *Metropolitan tabernacle pulpit.* London: Paternoster.

Stalker, J. 1891. *Life of Jesus Christ.* Chicago: Revell.

Stott, J. R. W. 1979. *Focus on Christ.* Cleveland: William Collins.

Strommen, M. P. 1974. *Five cries on youth.* New York: Harper and Row.

Thorson, W. R. 1969. In *The scientific enterprise and Christian faith,* ed. M. A. Jeeves. Downers Grove, Ill.: Inter-Varsity.

Tournier, P. 1962. *Guilt and grace.* New York: Harper and Row.

————. 1968. *A place for you.* New York: Harper and Row.

Tozer, A. W. 1955. *The pursuit of God.* Harrisburg, Pa.: Christian Publications.

Truax, C. B., and R. R. Carkhuff. 1967. *Toward effective counseling and psychotherapy.* Chicago: Aldine.

Van Til, C. 1940. *Articles on science.* Syllabus. Philadelphia: Westminster Theological Seminary.

—————. 1947. *Christian theistic ethics.* Syllabus. Nutley, N.J.: Presbyterian and Reformed.

—————. 1969. *A Christian theory of knowledge.* Philadelphia: Presbyterian and Reformed.

Viscott, D. 1976. *The language of feelings.* New York: Arbor House.

Wagemaker, H., Jr. 1978. *A special kind of belonging.* Waco, Tex.: Word.

Warfield, B. B. 1950. *The person and work of Christ.* Philadelphia: Presbyterian and Reformed.

White, E. 1955. *Christian life and the unconscious.* London: Hodder and Stoughton.

Wright, N. H. 1979. *Living with your emotions.* Irvine, Calif.: Harvest House.

Wuest, K. S. 1966. *Word studies in the Greek New Testament.* Vol. 1. Grand Rapids: Eerdmans.

Young, P. T. 1975. *Understanding your feelings and emotions.* Englewood Cliffs, N. J.: Prentice-Hall.

Index